Knots

Knots

Gordon Perry

whitecap

This book is produced by
Oceana Books
The Old Brewery
6 Blundell Street
London N7 9BH

ISBN 1-55285-823-5 and ISBN 978-1-55285-823-3

QUMK222

Manufactured in Hong Kong by
Modern Age Repro House Ltd.
Printed in China by
L. Rex Printing Co. Ltd.

Design and layout
by e-Digital Design

This book is intended for use as an introduction to knot tying. Readers are strongly advised to
seek advice from a qualified professional before using particular knots for climbing, rescue
work or dangerous activities that could result in personal injury or damage to equipment.
Please do not use this book if you are unwilling to assume the risk. For personalized advice,
please consult a qualified professional. The authors and publisher expressly disclaim
responsibility for any adverse effects arising from the use or application of the
information contained herein.

Contents

Introduction

"WHY KNOT?"
It's only a lump on a length of line,
A snarl in a piece of string.
But properly tied, by a practiced hand,
It becomes such a beautiful thing.

It is square. It is round. It can slip or hold fast.
That depends on the job that's required.
But when it's complete, all tucked in and neat,
It is really a sight to admire.

We splice it or hitch it. Make becket or bend.
Tie a grommet, an eye or a chain.
Make a sling or a sinnet, a noose or a net,
And none of them look quite the same.

Be it useful or fancy, for work or display,
If it's used once or twice or a lot,
There's nothing quite like it to make you feel proud,
Than knowing that you tied the knot.

The knots that I learned under canvas and pine,
At Scout camps in days long ago,
Are as handy today as they were in my youth,
But back then I just didn't know …

That those lumps on a line and those snarls in a string,
Would linger and not be forgot,
And foster a love for more knowledge and skill,
As I struggle to learn one more knot.

David Shaw

What better way to sum up the author's thoughts when writing this book?

As you progress through this book, the author hopes that you will gain a good basic understanding of knot tying and all that it involves. To lead you into the art of knotting, the book begins with a look at the many and varied types of ropes, lines, cords, and twines in production today. Understanding the characteristics of modern ropes is essential when it comes to "Safety," where "Strength, Security, and Suitability" will be your three main considerations in the selection of rope and the "right knot" for the job. Rope is also expensive and needs to be taken care of, not only in use, but also before and after.

Many "tools of the trade" are described to help the reader identify them, but of these only very few will be needed to complete the knots and splices in this book.

For the beginners, there is a gentle introduction to the "Foundations of Knotting," followed by a selection of the knots that get us through everyday life. Progressing to knots devised for more specific uses, the reader can then learn some splicing before advancing into the knots that we now tend to use more for our leisure and pleasure activities.

At the back of the book you will find a comprehensive glossary and a list of books and other sources where you will find more information on knot tying and allied skills.

Ropes, Tools, and Terminology

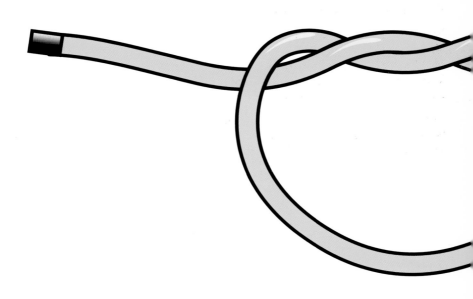

Rope Construction

Up to around a hundred years ago, most if not all rope was made from hemp, so the question of selection was not which rope, but how big. Currently, as there are so many different man-made fiber ropes to choose from, it is essential that any rope user has at least an insight into their characteristics.

Today's ropes are made up using three main methods of construction.

• **Stranded Rope**—Stranded (or twisted) rope is made up from the natural fibers of plants or from man-made filaments, called fibers. The "Fibers" are twisted into "Yarns," which in turn are twisted into "Strands," which are then laid up into three- or four-strand ropes. The "Lay" can be either "Right Hand," which is the normal method (spiraling upwards to the right), or "Left Hand." The twisting together of fibers in a right-handed direction, the strands left-handed and the rope right-handed, results in a "Right Hand Laid," or "Z" Laid Rope.

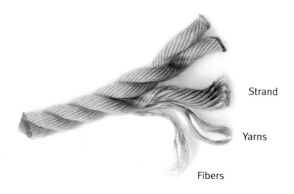

Strand

Yarns

Fibers

• **Multiplait Rope**—This is normally 8- or 12-strand rope and is made up by plaiting two (or three) pairs of left hand laid strands, with two (or three) pairs of right-hand laid strands. The result is a soft flexible rope that does not kink and is easy to stow.

• **Braided Rope**—Braids are made up of numerous combinations of cores, coats and covers of fine yarns, which are knitted singly or one over the other. Some braids are just a bare core, woven, braided or plaited. These are known as "Hollow Braid," "Solid Braid," 8, 12, 16 plait, etc. (not to be confused with Multiplait), or by their makers' trade names.

Others have a core that is protected or enhanced in strength by a cover, and in some cases the core is given a coat and then a cover. These are known as "Braid on Braid," "Double Braid," "Braid with 3 strand core," "Braid with parallel core," or by the manufacturer's trade names. Because some cores are difficult to handle (being so thin), or require protection from friction, they are often given an extra coat, either chemically or by wrapping with a bandage-like arrangement or bulking out with a woven coat.

Natural Fiber Ropes

Natural fiber ropes are not very prominent today; however, most are still available, especially sisal, cotton, and jute. Natural fiber ropes are made from the bast, seed, or leaf fibers of plants, which are stripped, dried, treated, and spun into yarns.

• **Hemp**—Made from the bast fibers of the *Cannabis sativa* plant, it is strong and soft to handle. Light brown to almost white in color, it was once used extensively in rigging old ships, but can still be found in theater rigging.

• **Manila**—Made from the leaf fibers of the abaca or wild banana plant, it is not as strong as hemp and can be hard on the hands. Golden brown in color, it is a "general purpose" rope.

- **Sizal**—Made from a cactus-like plant "agave," like Manila it is not as strong as hemp. Straw colored, it is an inexpensive general purpose rope that is still manufactured in many parts of the world.

- **Bass or Coir**—Made from the fibers of the coconut, which are soaked, beaten, and dried then spun into yarns. The weakest of rope size for size, it is normally soft laid, but rough on the hands. A dark golden brown in color, it floats in salt water and was once favored for berthing lines. It is now found mostly as outdoor barrier ropes or boat fenders.

- **Jute**—Made from the bast fibers of the Jute plant, it is now not normally seen in other than thin twines or cords. Mid-brown in color, soft in texture and to handle, it is used for such things as garden twine and braided sash cords.

- **Cotton**—Made from the fibers of the seed of the cotton plant, it is the weakest of all ropes, but still used extensively. White in color, cotton rope is very soft and nice to handle. Larger ropes are used for indoor rope barriers; cords and twines for decorative work and of course sewing threads.

Man-made Fiber Ropes

The most common man-made, or synthetic, fibers used in rope construction today are Polyamides, Polyester, Polypropylene, and Polythene.

• **Polyamides (PA)** – Commonly known as Nylon or Perlon, Nylon is strong with excellent stretching properties, although it does lose some strength when wet. Used in ropes where stretch or shock loading is likely, such as berthing hawsers, lifelines, and towropes.

• **Polyester (PES or PET)** – Commonly known as Terylene or Dacron, it is almost as strong as Nylon, but retains its strength when wet. It is hard wearing and does not stretch as much as Nylon. Often used together with Polypropylene as a rope cover.

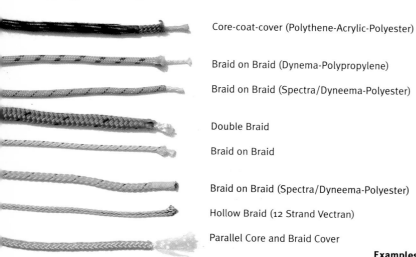

Core-coat-cover (Polythene-Acrylic-Polyester)

Braid on Braid (Dynema-Polypropylene)

Braid on Braid (Spectra/Dyneema-Polyester)

Double Braid

Braid on Braid

Braid on Braid (Spectra/Dyneema-Polyester)

Hollow Braid (12 Strand Vectran)

Parallel Core and Braid Cover

Examples of braided ropes

**Examples of hawser
laid or stranded ropes**

Nylon

Polyester 3 Strand

Polypropylene

Polyester (spun)

Spun Staple Polypropylene

Spun Staple Polypropylene

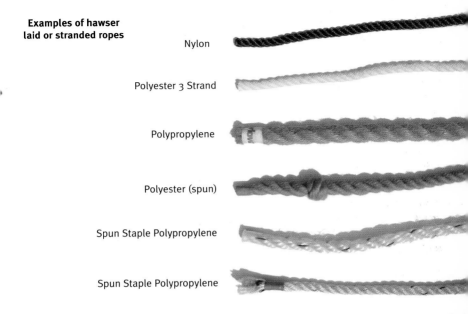

• **Polypropylene (PP)** – Used in its long fiber form, split film, spun
or fibrillated, Polypropylene is often used to make ropes that look like
natural fiber ropes. Split film ropes are very cheap and commonly
used to pull cables through ducting and for other uses where it can be
used and thrown away.

• **Polyethylene (PE)** – Made from white or colored fibers, Polyethylene
rope is very strong and will float. It is also the scientifically most
advanced material in rope making, producing many fiber variations
known collectively as High Modulus Polyethylene (HMPE) – size for
size, ropes in this group can be as strong as Steel Wire Rope. A note of
caution—HMPE is weakened considerably by knots and tight bending.

Care of Rope

Rope, cord, and line of any sort will serve you well, provided it is cared for—not just while in use, but before and after as well. Safety of life and limb, as well as goods and chattels, to say nothing of your pride, depends on how well you know, and have cared for, the rope you are using.

The following list of DOs and DON'Ts is not exhaustive, but will be a good starting point when learning to care for your rope.

DO

• Choose the right rope for the job—remember—HMPE ropes may be strong but they do NOT take kindly to being tied in knots.

• Remove rope from new coils with care—take rope from a drum or coil the way it was put on.

• Check Certification and History Sheets of Climbing Ropes before use.

• Check for damage before use.

• Keep rope clean. especially if exposed to salt water—wash with fresh water and a non-detergent type soap.

• Remove any knots when not in use.

• Coil ropes properly, according to the type of rope.

• Store coiled, hanging, clean, and dry.

DON'T
• Damage ropes with friction burns—these could be hidden inside a rope cover and prove dangerous if the rope is used.

• Damage ropes with oil, chemicals, sand or grit.

• Stand on or drop heavy loads on working ropes.

• Load a rope that has kinks or unintentional knots in it—they both weaken a rope considerably.

• Overload or overstretch ropes or bungee cord—this can cause permanent damage to the rope; eventually it will break and at worse cause an accident.

• Leave untreated ropes exposed to UV rays unnecessarily.

Tools for Ropework

Knots are generally tied without tools—although a few simple tools become necessary when tying complex knots and of course for splicing. The choice of tools, as with many other trades and hobbies, will depend on the type of work being tackled, and the craftsman's personal preference.

A Knife. A Jack Knife, similar to the one shown, here has been favored by sailors for many years. A blunt nose blade with a broad back (that will take a hammer blow) and a very sharp cutting edge is what makes a good rigger's knife.

A

B Scissors. Mainly used for cord and twines—the pair shown here are specialist scissors designed to cut through Spectra fibers.

B

C Hot Knife. A hot blade or wire is used to cut man-made fiber ropes, so that the ends seal. The pocket hot knife shown here is heated by gas (butane lighter fuel).

C

D Whipping Twine & Tape. Waxed twines are used for whipping, seizing, and sewing, while tape is normally used as a temporary stop when cutting or splicing ropes.

D

E

E **Swedish Fid.** A tapered steel fid, with a hollow shaft and small palm handle. Extremely useful for splicing and general ropework.

F

F **Wooden Fid.** A tapered wooden cone shaped tool, usually made from very hard woods. Used to open out the strands of twisted ropes when splicing.

G

G **Marlin Spike.** A tapered steel tool, used to open out the strands of wire ropes when splicing. Also useful to beat splicing into shape, act as a lever and undo shackles and clips.

H

H **Splicing Needles.** Splicing needles are used when splicing braided ropes. They vary in design and some are more versatile than others.

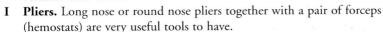

I **Pliers.** Long nose or round nose pliers together with a pair of forceps (hemostats) are very useful tools to have.

I

J   **Wire Loop.** These loops are normally home-made affairs, to suit the craftsman. Any stiff wire (piano wire, fence wire etc) formed into a loop can be glued into a tool handle, or bound and knotted over to provide a grip.

K   **Awl.** A small inexpensive awl, with a nice palm handle and the point slightly blunted and bent, makes a very useful tool for tightening up decorative knotting projects.

L   **Sewing Palm.** Used for pushing sewing needles through canvas and rope.

M   **Needles.** An assortment of "Sailmaker's" needles, packing and sack needles, as well as hollow needles, are necessary tools for the Palm and Needle whipping, splicing braided ropes and sewing ropes together.

N   **Heaving Mallet.** This looks much like a hammer, but it is not. The head is a fulcrum about which the handle rotates to act as a lever to tighten up strands in splices, or pull rope through tight apertures.

O   **Serving Boards.** Serving tools come in the shape of a mallets or boards. Both are used to serve small line tightly over a rope or rail.

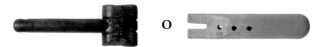

Foundations of Knotting

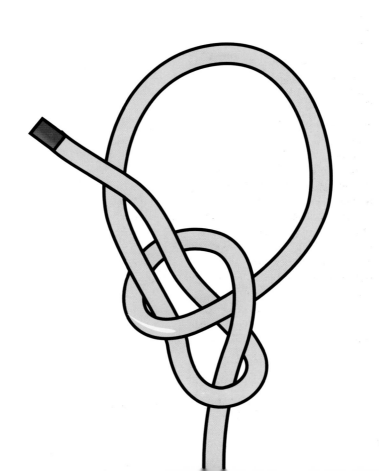

Introduction and Terminology

The terms used in this book are fairly standard, but language and translations do vary so do not be surprised if you come across people using others. The diagrams show how the parts of a rope are named, and explain the terminology used in this book for the parts of a knot. Other terms include the different names used to roughly describe cordage (a general term for all ropes), and finally those used when handling ropes and lines.

CORDAGE:

• **Rope**—All cordage over about $^1/_2$ inch (10 mm) is generally considered to be "rope." There are exceptions, particularly Flexible Steel Wire Rope.

• **Cord and Line**—These terms are used very loosely to describe thinner rope constructions and to prefix or suffix specific items such as "Piping Cord" and "Cod Line," etc. Fishing line and kite line are often very thin.

• **Twine**—Commonly called "string," twines are "small stuff," used for whipping, stops, sewing, and general use. Whipping twine, garden twine, and sailmaker's twine are the common ones.

PARTS OF A ROPE:

• **Standing Part**—That part of a rope that is fixed, under load or around which a knot is formed.

• **Working End**—The end of the rope that is used to "weave" the knot.

• **Bight**—Any part of the rope that forms or is used to form a loop that does not cross or join at any part.

• **Crossing Loop**—A complete circular loop formed by crossing the working end over or under the standing part.

• **Loop**—An eye formed by bringing two parts of a rope together side by side. A loop formed in a rope by a knot, splice or seizing.

• **Whipping**—The binding of rope with twine to prevent the strands from un-laying or the ends from fraying.

• **Seizing**—The joining of two ropes, or parts of a rope, by binding them together.

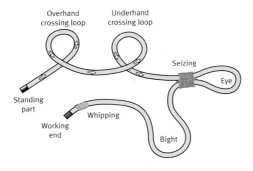

PARTS OF A KNOT AND TERMS:

• **Tuck:** The passing of the working end under another lead in a knot.

• **Belly:** The under-slung bight in a binding knot.

• **Nip:** The action of two or more parts of a knot that binds it so that it does not slip.

• **Collar:** A bight around the standing part or parts of a knot.

• **Lead:** The path(s) taken by a line through a knot.

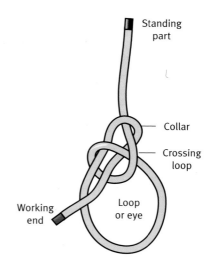

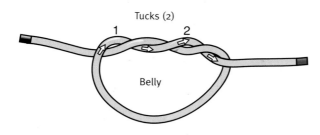

TERMS USED IN HANDLING ROPES:

• **Coil:** To wind a rope for stowage when not in use. Stranded (including twisted core braid) rope is coiled in a circle with the lay of the rope—other braided rope is coiled in a figure of eight to prevent kinking.

• **Hank:** To wind a coil of small line for stowage or ready use.

• **Cheese:** To form a spiral of rope on the deck.

• **Belay:** To make a rope fast to a fixture such as a cleat, bollard, rail, etc.

• **Secure:** To make fast a working rope so that it will stay in its present position.

• **Take a turn:** To pass a rope around an object once.

• **Take a round turn:** To pass a rope around an object a full 360°.

• **Take a crossing turn:** To pass a rope around an object then over its standing part to entrap it.

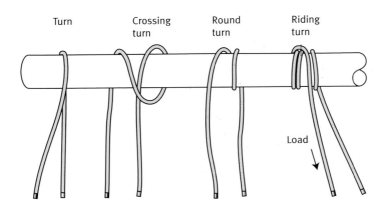

Turn   Crossing turn   Round turn   Riding turn

Load

Foundation Knots

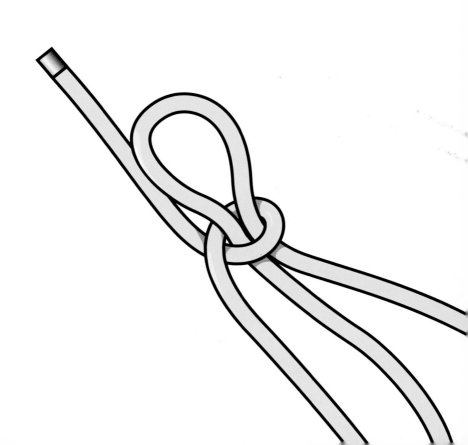

Introduction

This section is intended to sow the seeds of successful knot tying and is aimed at the newcomer to knotting who wants to learn from basics, or the person who learned a few knots many years ago who would like a little refresher course. Here you will find a gradual introduction, starting with the simplest of knot formations, which in turn will make up much more complicated knots as you progress through the book.

Starting with the Overhand and Half Knot structures and their variations—you might just be amazed at the number of knots that are made up of these in one form or another – the section ends with the basic knots that have been used, tried and tested over many years and will be familiar to most Scouts and Guides. For the decorative knotting enthusiast, these knots are equally important as they too form many of the knots used in Macramé and Marlinspike Work—a small taste of decorative knotting can be experienced as early as page 34.

Ideally, to practice the knots in this section you will need two lengths of line about ⁵/₁₆ inch (8 mm) diameter and not less than about 5 feet (1.5 meters) long—but if needs must a pair of long round shoe laces will suffice. One small length of 3-strand rope to practice the Wall and Crown knots—or you can tape three lengths of string together if necessary. A pencil or cardboard tube will suffice as a spar and you will be ready to go.

Overhand Knot *Also known as Thumb Knot*

The Overhand Knot, or Thumb Knot, as it is sometimes called, is a common factor in a large number of the knots that have been devised since man, and indeed birds and animals, started tying knots. As well as the Overhand Knot in its basic form, many variations and mutations of it will be referred to in a number of the knots in this book. It is normally tied in the end of a line as a Stopper Knot. However the applications it can be put to and number of uses seem unlimited.

Tie by holding the standing part of the line in one hand and with the other hand form a crossing loop (either right or left — it makes no difference) towards the working end; then tuck the working end through the loop as shown in the diagram.

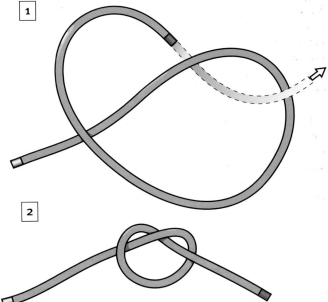

Slipped Overhand Knot

This knot is an introduction to "Slipped Knots"—those many and varied knots, which, because they may need to be untied easily or in a hurry, are formed with a bight close to the working end, so that when the working end is pulled the knot "spills" and comes undone. The Slipped Overhand Knot is a simple progression from the previous knot, which is also commonly used as a Stopper Knot tied in the end of a line—especially sewing cotton—as it makes a larger knot that can be easily untied by pulling on the working end. Like the Overhand Knot, it forms the basis of many of the knots found in this book.

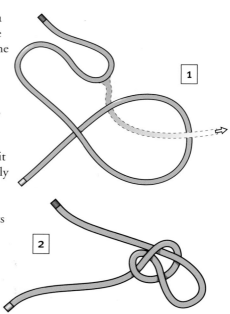

Tied in a similar manner to the Overhand Knot, except that instead of tucking the working end of the line through the loop, pull a bight from near the working end through the loop.

Overhand Loop

The Overhand Loop (fixed loop) is simply an Overhand Knot tied with a bight, by doubling the line either near the end or somewhere in the middle. Use with care and leave a long working end, especially in slippery line.

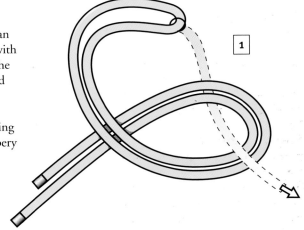

1

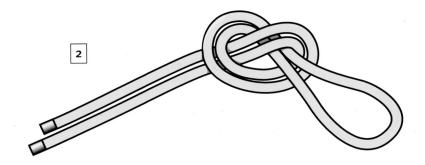

2

Overhand Noose

An Overhand Noose (sliding loop) is really an Overhand Knot tied in the working end around the standing part. Take care to learn the difference between this and the Slipped Overhand Knot.

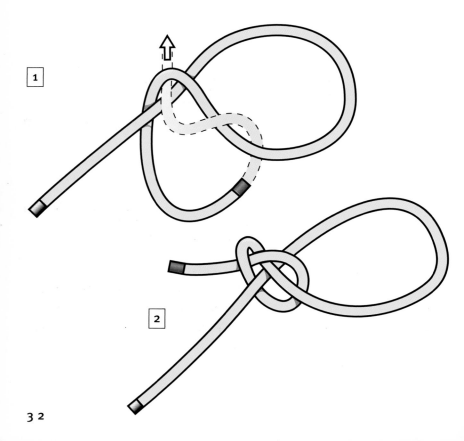

1

2

Double Overhand Knot

This is another knot that is used extensively in rope work and many knots rely on it either directly or as a method of securing the working end to prevent a knot from coming untied. Take a careful look at this method of tying and how the "belly loop" of the knot actually ends up forming the outer turns.

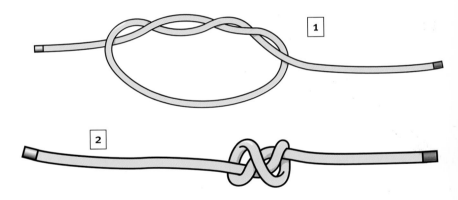

1

2

Tie it as you would an Overhand Knot but tuck the working end twice. Pull the ends slowly until the belly loop is snug on top of the two turns under it. You may need to tie this a few times before you get the knot to form correctly. This not only makes a nice stopper knot near the end of a line, but also a small knob at the top of a tassel in small diameter lines. A little later in the book you will learn how to tie this knot using the so called "grapevine" method.

Multiple Overhand Knots

Having seen how the Double Overhand Knot is formed you can now progress to multiple overhand knots and introduce yourself to elementary decorative knots—this one is popular at the end of waist cords for gowns etc.

The important thing to grasp when tying this knot is that you form a "belly loop" that is large enough to span all the tucks, as shown in diagram 1. The slipperiness of the surface of your line will determine how easy it is to pull this knot up snug and neat. When pulled up tight it will be difficult, or in some materials even impossible, to untie. Pull on both ends, gradually allowing the "belly loop" to twist naturally around the knot. If it will not pull up easily, give the outer turns a gentle push with both thumbs and forefingers towards the center.

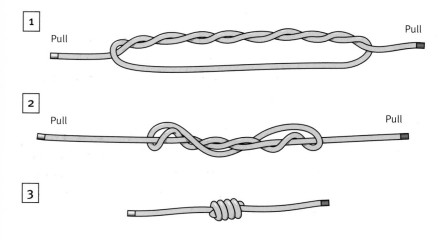

1   Pull   Pull

2   Pull   Pull

3

Half Hitch and Marlin Hitch

Another basic element in knot tying, the Half Hitch, is much used, but it is well to remember that it will not stand alone. In the diagram you will see two Half Hitches joined by a standing part—if you were to cut this, the knot would become nothing more than a "turn." Yet, together, these two Half Hitches form another knot (a Lark's Head) because one supports the other. Also, if one end of a line is secured, it is possible to use a number of Half Hitches from that point to form other knots or bindings.

To tie, tuck the working end under the standing part.

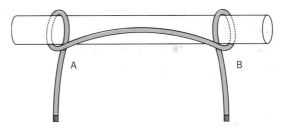

At first glance, the Marlin Hitch might look similar to the Half Hitch but there is an important difference—the Marlin Hitch has a holding property (because it is really an Overhand Knot in disguise). Like the Half Hitch, it is normally used with one end of the line secured.

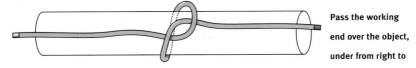

Pass the working end over the object, under from right to left, then over the standing part and tuck, pull down and away to tighten it, then bring the working end up at right angles to the turn, and repeat as necessary.

Slipped Hitches

The Slipped Half Hitch is nothing
more than a Slipped Overhand Knot
tied around an object.

To tie, take a turn with the working end and tuck a
bight from the working end between the turn and
the object.

1

This is a handy knot to take the weight of an
attended line, like a fender lanyard, temporarily.

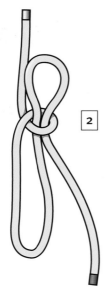

2

Another useful application of the Half Hitch is
shown in the second diagram—this one is
known as the Bell Ringer's Hitch and as well as
being useful to keep the bell rope off the
ground when not in use, this knot is the start
of the very popular Trucker's Hitch (page 134).

To tie, gather up one or more bights in the rope and form a
Half Hitch around them as shown in the diagram.

Half Knots and Square Knot

The Half Knot is probably the first knot we learn as a child, as it forms the base of the knot we use to tie our shoe laces. It is in fact an Overhand Knot that is tied around an object or by using two working ends. However this is another knot that is rarely left to stand alone and one that needs another knot to stop it from coming undone. By using two Half Knots together we can form a well known binding knot, the Square Knot.

Tie by passing the working ends, right over left, tuck and pull, left over right, tuck and tie.

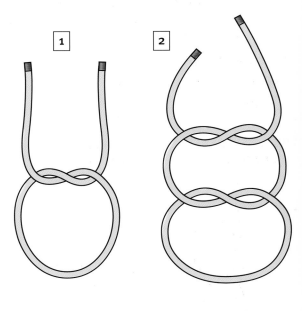

Slipped Half Knot

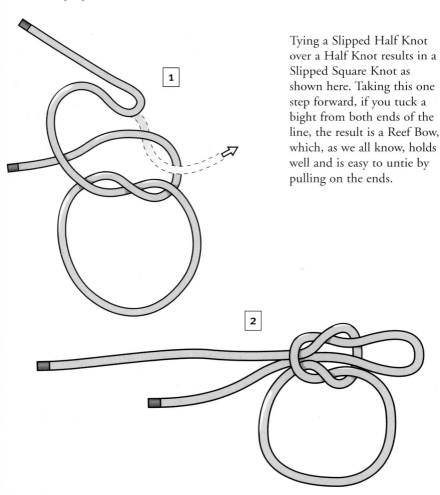

Tying a Slipped Half Knot over a Half Knot results in a Slipped Square Knot as shown here. Taking this one step forward, if you tuck a bight from both ends of the line, the result is a Reef Bow, which, as we all know, holds well and is easy to untie by pulling on the ends.

Round Turn

Although not really a knot, making turns about an object plays a vital role in controlling, securing, and handling ropes and lines. The amount of friction created between the rope and the object increases with each turn, thus with a Turn, where the rope goes around the object and back, it is necessary to apply the same force to each end to stop it from moving. By adding another pass around the object you now have a Round Turn with more friction, which now requires less effort to hold a load applied to one end.

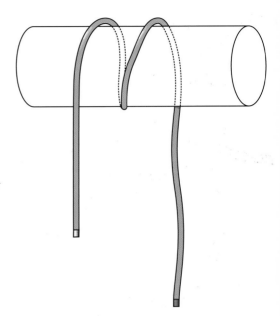

Additional turns will of course apply more friction and lessen the effort even more. However, too many turns may prevent the load from being "paid out." Care should also be taken not to let the end with the load ride up over the turns—this results in a Riding Turn, which not only prevents the load from being paid out, but can cause extensive friction damage to the rope, especially on a revolving winch drum.

Crown Knot

Yet another knot that is used as a foundation knot is the Crown Knot. Crowning is used to start a Back Splice in 3- or 4-strand rope and, as you will see in the closing chapters of this book, it is also used extensively in decorative knotting where Continuous Crowning (crowns on crowns) forms a sinnet or covering. Shown here is the start of a Back Splice in 3-strand rope.

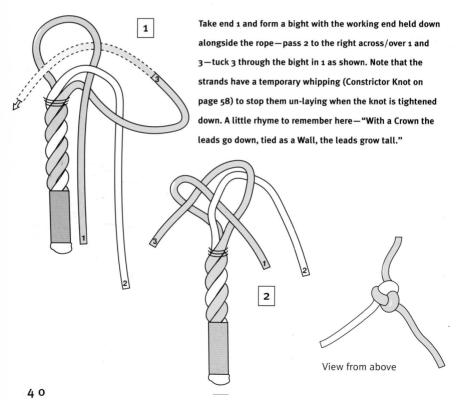

1 Take end 1 and form a bight with the working end held down alongside the rope—pass 2 to the right across/over 1 and 3—tuck 3 through the bight in 1 as shown. Note that the strands have a temporary whipping (Constrictor Knot on page 58) to stop them un-laying when the knot is tightened down. A little rhyme to remember here—"With a Crown the leads go down, tied as a Wall, the leads grow tall."

2

View from above

Wall Knot

The Wall Knot can be looked upon as an upside down Crown Knot and is used as a foundation for other knot forms, particularly in decorative knotting.

Shown here is the start of a Manrope Knot, which starts with the Wall Knot and has a Crown Knot tied over it.

Pass lead 1 under lead 2, pass lead 2 under 3, then tuck lead 3 through the bight formed in 1.

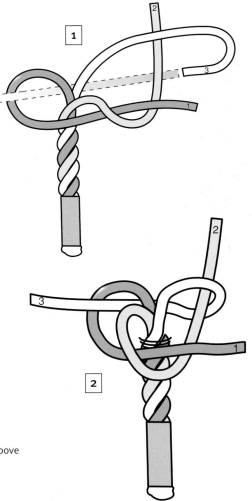

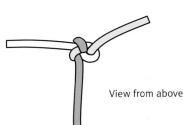

View from above

Everyday Knots

Clove Hitch

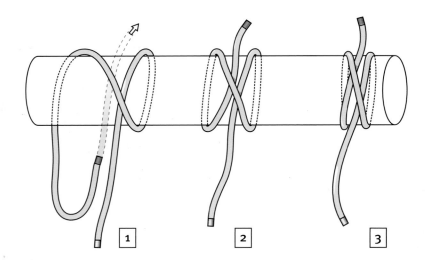

Another tried and tested knot that more often than not is used to secure the end of a rope to something. It is no more than two Half Hitches put together and in a later chapter you will see different methods of forming this knot.

To tie, make a turn with the working end around the object, bring the working end up to cross the standing part on the object, pass round the object once more and tuck the end under itself—adjust, then pull both ends to snug the knot up tight. Leave a long end, because if the knot is turned around the object it can unwind and come undone. The final tuck can be a bight instead of the working end, resulting in a Slip Clove Hitch, useful for securing a fender lanyard to a guardrail.

Clove Hitch (over a post)

Although there is nothing wrong with tying a Clove Hitch around a post using the method shown on the previous page, there is an easier way, if the top of the post (or other vertical object) is free.

Cast a Half Hitch (with the working end over the standing part) over the post, then by twisting the working end clockwise in your hand and at the same time moving your hand to the left, form a crossing loop (Half Hitch) and drop that over the post on top of the first one. Pull both ends to tighten, leaving a long working end.

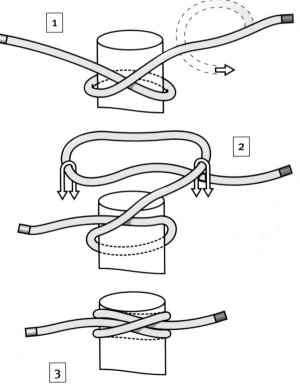

Clove Hitch (on a ring)

When securing a rope to a ring using a Clove Hitch.

Pass the working end through the ring, and to the right of the standing part. Cross the working end over the standing part and through the ring again. Now take the working end under itself and pull on both ends to tighten. Once again leave a long end or put two Half Hitches in the working end around the standing part.

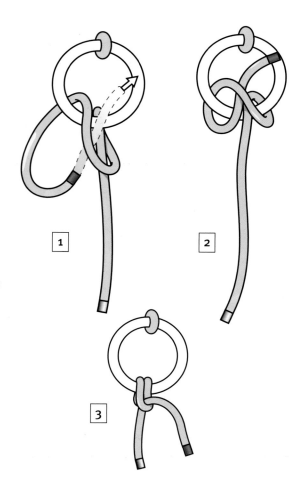

1

2

3

Round Turn and Two Half Hitches

Probably one of the most used and reliable knots, the Round Turn and Two Half Hitches is a combination of the Round Turn, which holds the load, using friction between the rope and the rail, and two Half Hitches, which stop the turns from slipping.

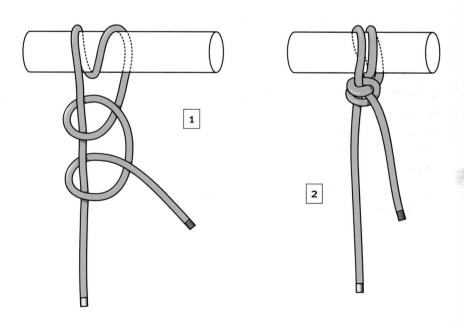

1

2

Pass the rope twice around the rail/ring/post, adjust the turns to hold the load, then apply two Half Hitches with the working end over the loadbearing standing part.

Figure of Eight Knot

If I could only teach a person one knot before sending them on an adventure, this would be it. Easy to tie, but not always to untie—easy to remember, as it ties like an 8. The versatility of the Figure of Eight Knot is boundless, as you will discover while working though the pages of this book. But for now we will concentrate on the basic knot and its use as a Stopper Knot.

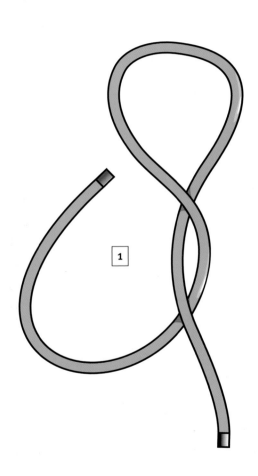

1

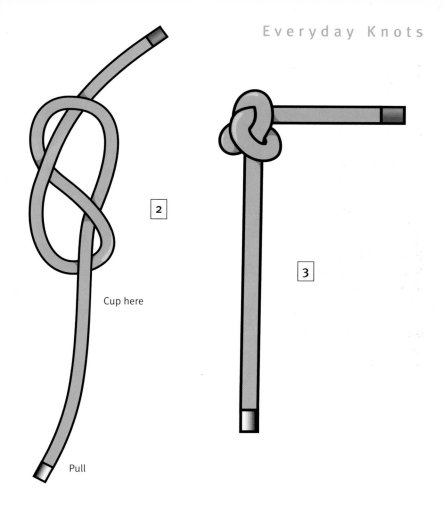

2

Cup here

Pull

3

Make a crossing loop, pass the working end around the standing part and back through the loop.

Pull on both sides of the knot to dress it, then tighten by cupping the knot in one hand and pulling on the standing part with the other—forming a knot that looks like the one in the diagram.

Square Knots (and Variations)

The Square Knot, in its basic form, is used to tie the two ends of a line when used as a binding. It should not normally be used as a bend, to join two ropes together, as it can easily slip or capsize into a Lark's Head (which is the normal method of untying a Square Knot that has been under stress) and fall apart. The beauty of this knot is that it lies flat, making it ideal to secure the ends of bandages—it is also used extensively in Macramé.

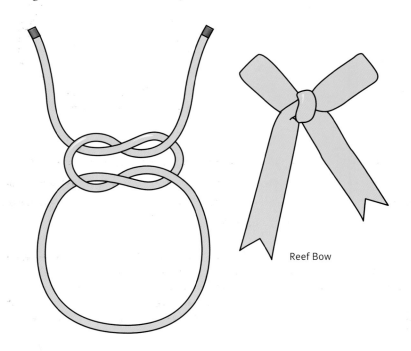

Reef Bow

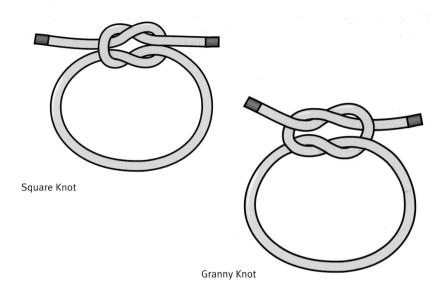

Square Knot

Granny Knot

The Square Knot is tied by using two Half Knots, one over the other, but the second must be tied the opposite way to the first. An easy way to remember this is to tie the working ends ... Right over left, tuck and tie, left over right, tuck and pull. If both Half Knots are tied the same way the result is a Granny Knot, which is neither as secure nor as neat when pulled up.

The Reef Bow Knot is used to tie shoe laces, to make bows for adornment or for tying ribbon—sailors have used this for years to tie their cap ribbons and tapes. Again it is important that the two Half Knots are tied the opposite way, otherwise the bow appears twisted to the left or right. Look at people's shoes—if the bow goes neatly across the shoe it is a Reef Bow, if it goes up and down the shoe it is a Granny Bow.

Common Bowline

The common Bowline is probably still the most used knot for forming a temporary fixed loop in the end of a line. Uses include forming fixed loops at the end of a mooring line, climbing lines, and for tying off such knots as the Oklahoma Hitch.

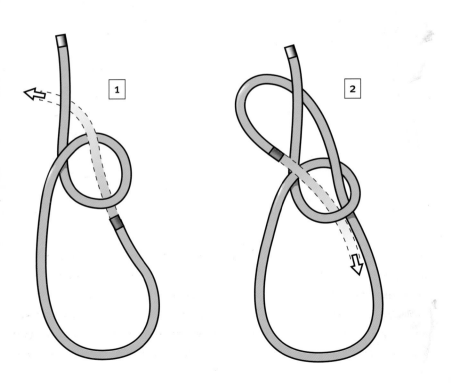

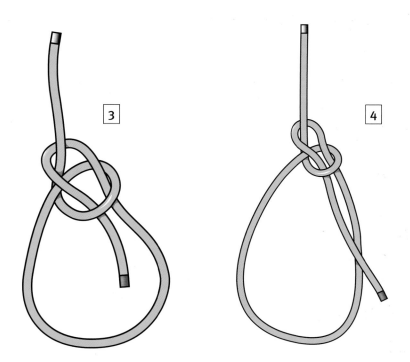

To tie this knot, form a closed loop (as you would write a figure 6) in the standing part, then pass the working end up through that loop, around the back of the standing part and down through the loop, and back alongside itself. Pull on both the standing part and the working end and loop to tighten the knot.

If a bowline becomes jammed tight, it can be untied by laying the standing part of the rope down alongside the working end in the loop, then pulling the collar around the standing part down towards the working end also. Variations of the Bowline and different tying methods will be found in the chapter on Loops & Nooses.

Sheet Bend

Being quick and easy to tie, the Sheet Bend is put to many and varied uses, particularly in joining two ropes that are of different diameters. This knot is only reliable when it is loaded. Although it will stay tied when not under load, it can become slack; therefore it should be checked and if necessary be pulled up again before use.

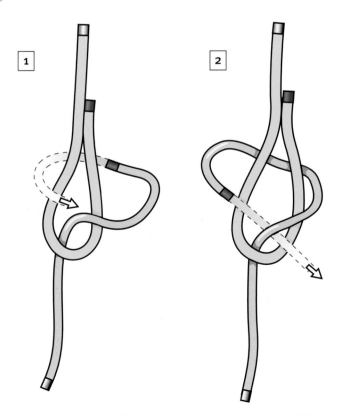

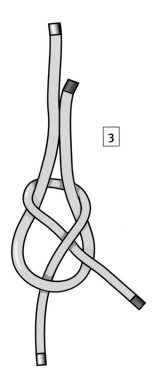

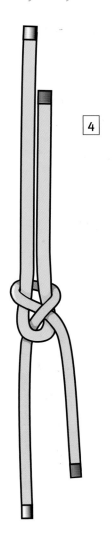

To tie, take the larger diameter rope and make a bight near the end—pass the working end of the other rope up through the bight, in the direction shown in diagrams 1 and 2, around the two parts of the thicker rope and back under itself. Pulling on both lines then sets the knot up tight, and provided it is under constant load it will remain so. Other methods of tying this knot, more suited to specific tasks, are shown later in this book.

Sheepshank

Although the Sheepshank has been in the Scouting repertoire for many years, it is probably the least used of the everyday or common knots. It has two traditional uses, one to incapacitate a damaged portion of a rope that needs to be used and the other to shorten a line without having to cut it. Shown here are two methods of tying, the first is suited to the damaged rope.

Make three closed loops as shown in diagram 1, making sure the damaged portion is in the center loop, pull the sides of the center loop through the outer two loops as shown, then pull on the ends to tighten the knot. The second method is more suited to long or larger ropes that may be too large to be tied using loops. Lay out a "Z" in a suitable part of the rope, form a Half Hitch as shown in diagram 3 and pass both bights of the "Z" through them before pulling the ends tight.

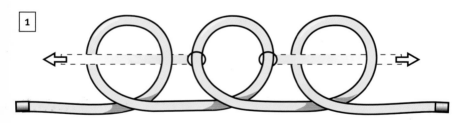

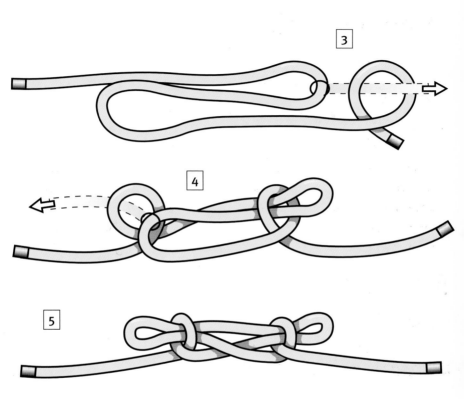

Be warned—this knot will come undone if it is not under constant load, therefore if you wish to make this a semi-permanent arrangement, the two ends must be either passed through the outer bights, or the outer bights and the standing parts seized together.

Constrictor Knot

To the rigger, tradesman, knotting enthusiast, and model maker, the Constrictor Knot is that knot which substitutes for the third hand we all so often need. Only really suited for use with lines of small diameters, it has the ability to be pulled up very tight and will normally hold so well that it has to be cut to untie it.

As a temporary whipping, for tying down a cloth cover over a jar or clamping items while glue dries—plus a hundred and one other uses—this knot is an absolute must in any knot tyer's repertoire.

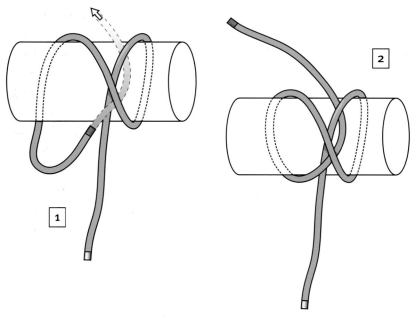

3

To tie, start as you would for the Clove Hitch—pass a crossing turn around the object and bring the working end up in front. Now pass the working end over the standing part then under it (forming a Half Knot under the crossing part) and pull both ends up. When you have arranged the object and knot to where you want them (remember you may only be able to undo this by cutting it), then pull both ends up as tight as necessary. Unlike most other knots these ends can be cut quite short and the knot will still hold. You will find more about this knot and some variations in the "Knots for Binding and Holding" chapter.

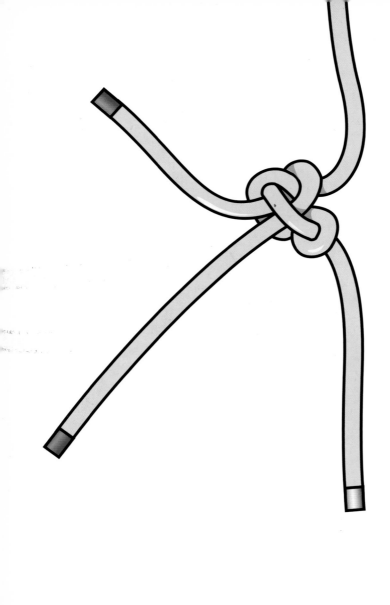

Knots Used to Join Ropes

Introduction

In this section you will find a selection of the knots commonly used in a wide range of pursuits to join ropes together. It is worth noting now that some of these knots may well be recommended for use in situations where the safety of life is involved—here you learn to tie the knot, but before you put it to use, you should have professional instruction.

Every knot in this section is made up of one or more of the knots learned in the Foundations chapter—Overhand Knots, Half Knots, Loops, and Turns.

Don't stop at learning a knot—when you have mastered the knots using your training ropes, it is a good idea to try each knot in very thin, thick and very thick ropes to see how they perform.

Then adventure into the slippery monofilaments, the nylons and the very hairy ropes to see how they each affect the tying and security of the various joining knots.

List of Knots and Uses

Fisherman's Knot

One of the easiest and most effective ways of tying two pieces of line together is to use the Fisherman's Knot. Although strictly speaking this is a "bend," it is termed a knot because there is, as you will discover later, also a Fisherman's Bend which is quite different.

Lay the two lines together, with one end to the left, the other to the right. Take one end and pass it around the standing part of the other line and tie an Overhand Knot as shown. Take the other end and make an identical knot in that around the standing part of the first line. Take care to make sure that the ends protrude as shown in the diagram; otherwise the two Overhand Knots will not sit snugly together when you pull on the two standing parts to draw the knot up tight.

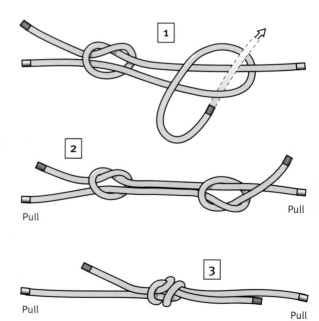

6 4

Double Fisherman's Knot

Like the Fisherman's Knot, the Double Fisherman's Knot is used to join the ends of two lines. However, because it is stronger and more reliable, it is better suited to join the ends of a rope when making a sling or strop. Because we cannot tie the double overhand knot using the method previously shown in this book, we have to employ what is known as the "grapevine method."

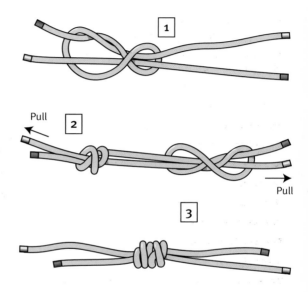

Lay the two ropes parallel, with their working ends in opposite directions. Tuck the first working end under the second rope and bring it back over both the second rope and itself. Still working back towards the standing part, tuck the working end under the standing part and the second line again.

Now pass the working end under the first crossing and then around the standing part to form an Overhand Knot. Pull up on the working end and the standing part to tighten. Now take the second line and repeat the process as shown. Tighten the second Double Overhand and then pull on the two standing parts to snug the knot together.

Figure Eight Bend *Also known as Flemish Bend*

The Figure Eight Bend, also known as the Flemish Bend, can be used to reliably join ropes of similar thickness.

Make a Figure of Eight Knot near the end of the first rope and then pass the working end of the second rope through the knot in the opposite direction parallel to and on the same side as the first Figure of Eight, until it emerges alongside the standing part of the first rope. Tighten by working the knot together so that both knots lie neat and snug together.

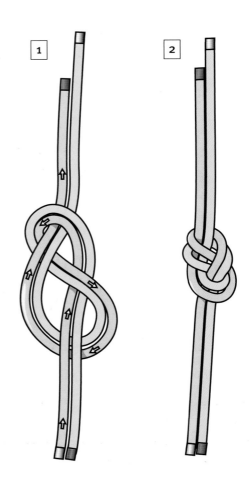

Fisherman's Eight Bend

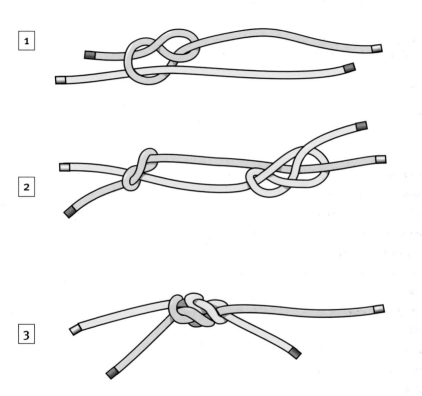

Another method of tying two lines together using the Figure of Eight Knot is shown here as the Fisherman's Eight Knot. This is tied in the same way as the Fisherman's Knot, only instead of using Overhand Knots, use Figure of Eight Knots. Once again make sure the ends lie as in the diagrams, otherwise the knot will not pull up snug.

Water Knot

Easily tied and quick to inspect for safety, the Water Knot, or Tape Knot or Ring Knot as it is sometimes called, is ideal for use in rope or webbing tape. It is used extensively by climbers to make up nylon webbing slings.

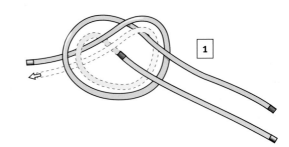

To tie, form an Overhand Knot in one end of the rope or tape (leaving an end of at least three to four times the diameter of the rope or width of the tape), then feed the other end back through the knot from the direction of the first knot's working end. If webbing tape is being tied, insure the tapes lie flat against each other all the way through the knot. Dress the knot, then pull tight—the ends can be taped to the standing parts to keep them in place and avoid snagging.

Strap Bend

As its name implies, the Strap Bend is especially suited to join leather straps or strips of banding etc. It can also be used to join springy materials like wire and thin strips of wood or plant fibers.

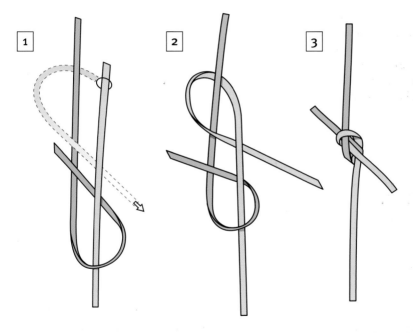

To tie, form a crossing loop with one end; pass the other end up through this and around the standing part of the first loop. Bring the end down under itself to form a Half Hitch and then pull the knot up so that the straps lie snug against each other. Leave fairly long ends, especially if using slippery material.

Sheet Bends and Alternatives

In addition to the Sheet Bend that featured in the section on Everyday Knots, there are three other useful Sheet Bend variants: the Slipped Sheet Bend (diagram1), Double Sheet Bend (diagram 2), and One Way Sheet Bend (diagrams 3 and 4).

The Slipped Sheet Bend is useful for passing lines where the recipient has only one hand free to undo the knot, or where a line may have to be slipped in an emergency, such as a tow line. Remember that, like the Sheet Bend, it needs to be loaded to be secure and therefore is not suitable for use in any life support rig.

The Double Sheet Bend is more secure than the single, and is better if the two ropes are of very different thickness. When tying, insure that the working end is passed under the standing part of the smaller line when going around the larger loop/bight. More than two turns can be used if necessary.

1

2

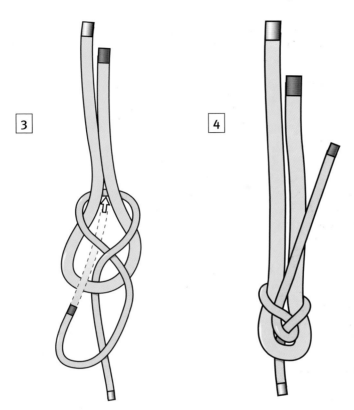

The One Way Sheet Bend is used where a larger line has to be passed through an aperture or fairlead, or over an obstruction. It can also be used to pull cables through ducting with a mouse line.

By tucking the working end of the hauling rope back through itself to lie alongside the hauled rope, you will ensure that it will not snag on any obstructions.

Heaving Line Bend

The Heaving Line Bend is used to attach a heaving line to a hawser or messenger.

Make a bight in the end of the hawser, then pass the heaving line first around the standing part side of the bight, then under itself and the other side of the bight. Bring it back across the bight and tuck under the turn around the standing part, as shown.

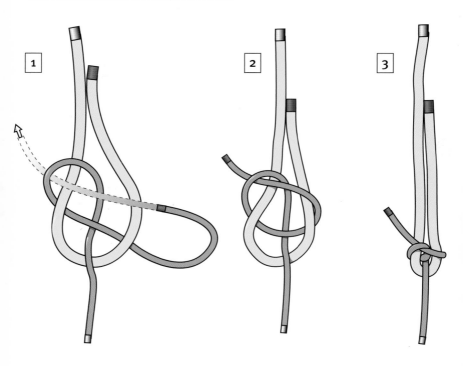

1

2

3

Racking Bend

When attaching a line or messenger to a large rope or wire hawser, it may be necessary to use a Racking Bend, to pull the sides of the hawser bight together to stop it from springing out.

Pass the line through the bight in the hawser in a snake-like manner as illustrated. Pull each turn up taut after each pass and secure the last one with a Half Hitch as shown.

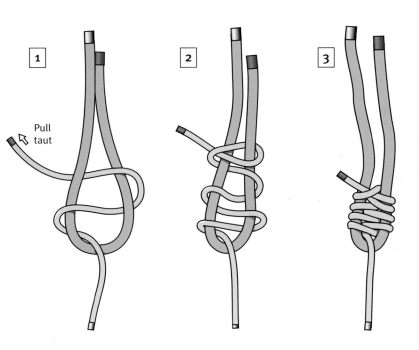

Pull
taut

1

2

3

Carrick Bend

Originally devised to join heavy hawsers so that they will pass around a capstan, the Carrick Bend is also useful in other applications, as you will discover later in the book.

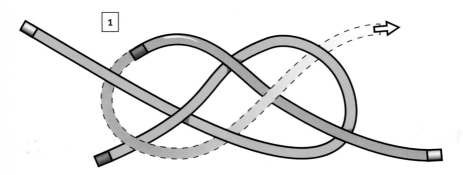

In large hawsers, lay the first rope end into a crossing loop as shown in diagram 1. Lay the second rope across this loop, then tuck the working end in an "under, over, under" sequence through the knot as shown by the arrowed line.

Note that the two working ends emerge on opposite sides of the knot. For added security, and to prevent snagging, the working ends are seized to the standing part as shown in diagram 3.

In smaller lines or rope, if the standing ends are pulled a knot will form like that shown in diagram 4.

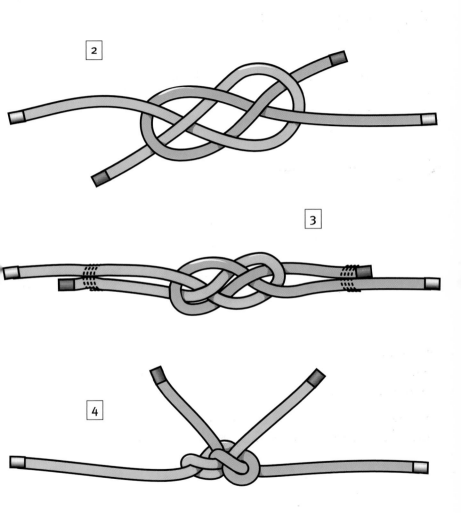

Blood Knot

Used primarily to join fishing lines of monofilament, the Blood Knot can be tricky to tie, and virtually impossible to untie. Before starting to tie this knot in monofilament line it is advisable to have a clothes peg or bulldog clip handy.

Lay the two lines parallel with the working ends in opposite directions, and then with one line make between four and six turns around the standing part of the second line.

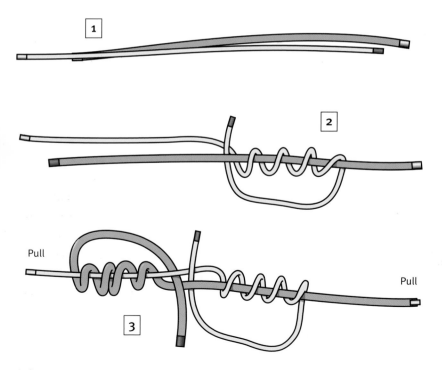

1

2

Pull

Pull

3

Bring the working end back to the start of the turns (leaving a belly loop) and pass it between its own standing part and the second line as illustrated—hold this in place with your clip. Now take the working end of the second line and make the same number of turns around the standing part of the first line, feeding the working end back into the center of the knot, but in the opposite direction to the first.

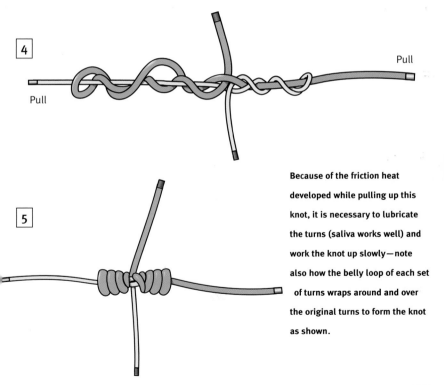

4

Pull

Pull

5

Because of the friction heat developed while pulling up this knot, it is necessary to lubricate the turns (saliva works well) and work the knot up slowly—note also how the belly loop of each set of turns wraps around and over the original turns to form the knot as shown.

Ashley's Bend

Clifford Ashley does not name this bend in his book; he just says it is probably original and numbers it 1452, but it has become so popular that rather than being referred to as "The Ashley Book of Knots Bend #1452," it is now known simply as Ashley's Bend. It can be used in almost any line, or even in bungee cord. It is easy to learn to tie and will take a load on any one or combinations of its standing or working ends, without coming untied; even after loading it can be untied without too much effort.

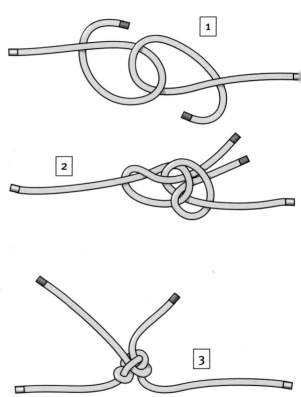

To tie, lay the two lines with their working ends overlapping, then make a closed loop with both working ends as shown in diagram 1. Bring the two working ends together and pass them through the center aperture of the two loops as shown in diagram 2. Dress the knot and pull up tight.

Rigger's Bend *Also known as Hunter's Bend*

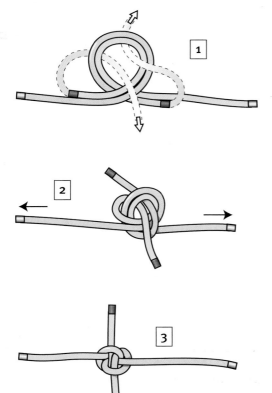

The next knot, Hunter's Bend or the Rigger's Bend, performs a similar function and is also named after a person, Dr Hunter, although it was later discovered that he had in fact not been the first person to publish its existence.

Lay the two lines together with their working ends in opposite directions, then form a crossing loop, with both lines held together as shown in diagram 1. Now pass the working ends in opposite directions through the center of this loop, dress the knot and pull up tight with the standing parts.

79

Loops and Nooses

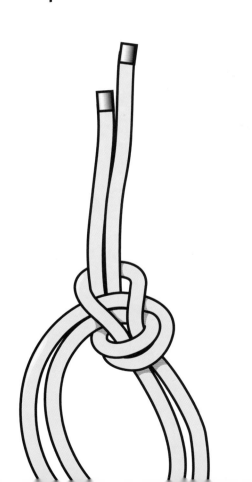

Introduction

The following selection of loops and nooses will provide the reader with a good cross section of both fixed and sliding loops. Many of these are used by anglers, climbers, sailors, model makers, and for many of the popular outdoor pursuits.

Some of these can be dangerous, so great care should be taken that they are not used in life threatening situations without proper training. Remember, this book is intended to show how to tie the knots and cannot possibly cover all the security, reliability, safety, and suitability factors associated with these knots.

Again you will find that the Overhand Knot and its variants feature often in this section, and although some of the knots may look and have names that sound quite daunting, if you have covered the basics, they will be quite easy to learn.

List of Knots and Uses

GENERAL PURPOSE

SLIPPED OVERHAND LOOP—Make a temporary loop that can be slipped easily. **Page 85**

POACHER'S NOOSE—Form a loop that will slide and grip. **Page 92**

RUNNING BOWLINE—Hoist or lower an inanimate object. **Page 106**

PORTUGUESE BOWLINE—Form a knot with two adjustable loops. **Page 108**

SPANISH BOWLINE—Form two fixed loops to suspend articles from. **Page 110**

HANDCUFF KNOT—Make a hobble for the legs of a large animal. **Page 112**

TOM FOOL KNOT—Form a "Fireman's Chair" for light rescue. **Page 113**

LANYARD LOOP KNOT—Make a decorative loop for knife or whistle lanyard. **Page 118**

FISHING

FISHERMAN'S LOOP—Tie an adjustable loop in monofilament or slippery line. **Page 94**

DOUBLE OVERHAND LOOP—Tie a fixed loop in monofilament or slippery line. **Page 84**

ANGLER'S LOOP—Quick and easy fixed loop, or leader loop. **Page 88**

BLOOD LOOP DROPPER KNOT—Small loop in monofilament fishing rig. **Page 116**

CAMPING & CLIMBING

FIGURE OF EIGHT LOOP—Fixed loop that can be tied in a bight or in the end of a rope. **Page 86**

HONDA LOOP—Sliding loop knot, suitable for bowstrings or a lasso. **Page 90**

MANHARNESS LOOP—Form a hand-hold or shoulder loop with which to haul a rope. **Page 91**

SWAMI LOOP—Make a reliable adjustable fixed loop. **Page 96**

BOWLINE (CLIMBER'S)—Method of forming a fixed loop around a remote object. **Page 98**

TUCKED BOWLINE—Uses the Yosemite tie off to make it more secure and keep the end out of the loop. **Page 102**

ALPINE BUTTERFLY LOOP—Line loop, which is fixed and can be tied in a bight or the end of a line. **Page 114**

SLIDING DOUBLE FISHERMAN'S LOOP —Adjustable sling or decorative curtain holdback. **Page 120**

BOATING

BOWLINE (COMMON)—Fixed loop in the end of a rope. **Page 98**

WATER BOWLINE—Bowline that is easier to untie after it has been under load. **Page 100**

BOWLINE ON A BIGHT—Tie a fixed loop in the bight of a rope. **Page 104**

Double Overhand Loop

Also known as Gut Knot

Primarily used to form a loop in the end of a monofilament fishing line, the Double Overhand Loop, or Gut Knot, is also equally at home in thin wire, light line or cord.

It is tied by doubling the end of a line, and tying a Double Overhand Knot in the doubled end. When using springy line, it helps to tie the knot around the index finger, making it easier to hold the turns with the adjacent thumb.

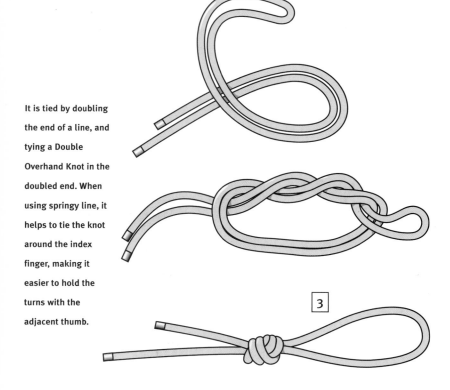

84

Slipped Overhand Loop

The Slipped Overhand Loop is a useful way in which to form a temporary fixed loop (that can easily be slipped), from a noose.

Tie a slipped Overhand Knot to form the noose, adjust the loop to the required size and apply a Slipped Half Hitch with the working end over the standing part. The knot can be quickly released by pulling on the working end.

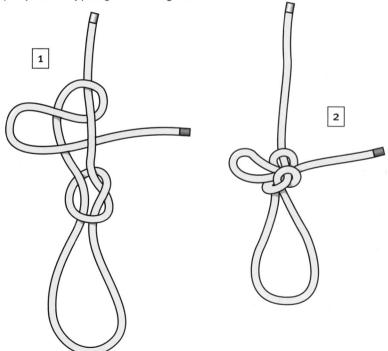

Figure of Eight Loop

Equally as good as a Bowline, but requiring more line to tie, is the Figure of Eight Loop. In fact some people call this a Figure of Eight Bowline, as it is after all a knot forming a fixed loop.

Shown here are two methods by which this knot can be tied. Firstly if the loop is to be used free, to tie in to a harness or karabiner etc—double the rope where the loop is required, or double back the end; the bight at the end of the loop is now treated as the working end, which is tied as a Figure of Eight Knot as shown.

Adjust the size of the loop as required, then pull up the knot, being careful to keep the two lines at equal tension and lying parallel alongside each other.

The second method of tying is used when the line acts as a Hitch to a spar, ring or other object where a fixed loop cannot be put over or clipped into. Form a Figure of Eight Knot very loosely in the standing part of the rope, leaving a very long end. Pass the working end around the object to which it is being secured, then feed it back through the Figure of Eight as shown the diagram.

Tighten by pulling on the standing part and adjacent working end, again being careful to keep equal tension and the two lines parallel while drawing the knot up tight.

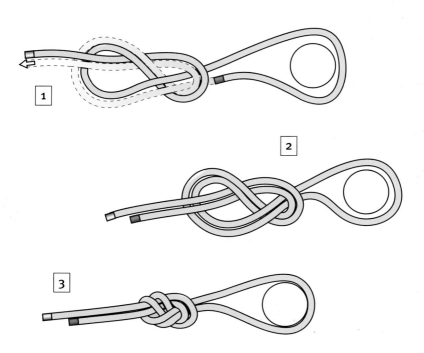

Angler's Loop *Also known as Perfection Loop*

Also known as the Perfection Loop, the Angler's Loop is a reliable and easily tied knot, but in some materials is difficult to untie after it has been under load. Its primary use is to form a leader loop used by anglers to connect the leader to a casting line; however, I have seen it used in rope and lines for many other uses, even for mooring fishing vessels.

There are two other knots that are similar in structure, and equally efficient, namely the so-called "Tugboat" or "Flying Bowline" and the Algonquin Bowline—however, there are differences and care should be taken not to mistake one for the other.

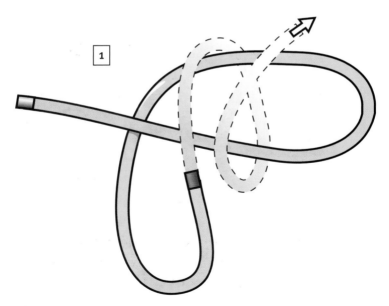

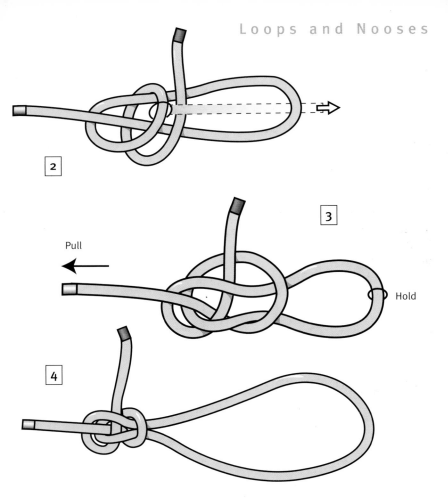

2

3

Pull

Hold

4

Make a crossing loop as shown in diagram 1, then make a loose turn around that loop to form the structure in diagram 2. Now pull the loose turn over the working end and through the first loop. Tighten the knot by pulling on the standing part and the resulting loop.

Honda Loop *Also known as Bowstring Knot*

Here is an example of how two simple Overhand Knots are used to provide a useful knot. The Honda Loop or Bowstring Knot forms a round loop in the end of a rope, making it suitable as a lasso or lariat knot. The first part of the knot is the Bowstring Knot, and as its name implies it was used to attach one end of a bow string to a longbow.

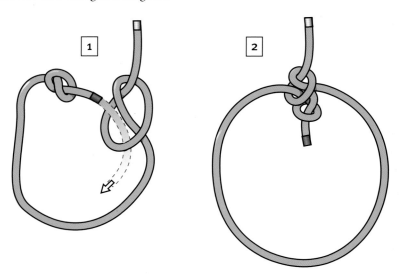

Tie an Overhand Knot in the standing part, leaving enough line to form the loop. Tie an Overhand Stopper Knot in the working end. Pass the working end through the Overhand Knot as shown in diagram 1 making sure that it passes under the standing part of the Overhand, otherwise it will not have the required grip. Adjust the loop for size, move the end Overhand Knot as necessary to maintain that size and snug it up as shown in the diagram.

Manharness Loop *Also known as Artillery Hitch*

The Manharness Loop or Artillery Hitch provides a hand hold or, if made large enough, a shoulder loop, so that a rope can be hauled more easily than with a hand grip around the rope.

The knot can be tied either near the end of the rope or some way along it therefore it is normal to tie it "in the bight." Make a crossing loop in the line and tuck one side under the right-hand standing part as shown the diagram. Now take the belly of the bight and pass it over that same standing part and under itself as shown in the diagram.

Pull up using both standing parts, adjusting the loop to a suitable size in the process.

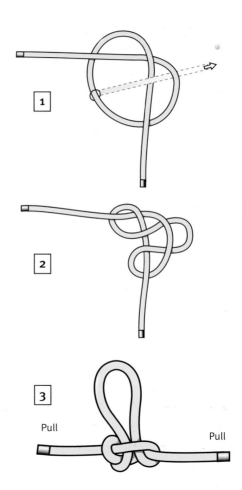

91

Poacher's Noose *Also known as Double Overhand Noose*

One of my favorite knots, the Poacher's Noose, or Double Overhand Noose, (or if tied with a Triple Overhand Knot it becomes a Scaffold Knot), is another one of those ever-useful "third hand" knots.

The knot can be made to slide freely or to hold firm and could no doubt be used as a snare knot by poachers, but it has many more uses. It can be used to temporarily hold a hard eye in the end of a rope, or even act as a clamp when gluing, because the loop can take a considerable amount of pressure and hold quite firm.

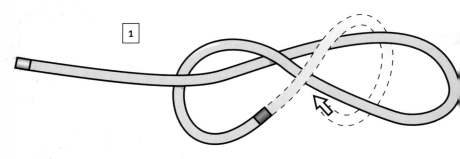

It is tied using the grapevine method of tying the Double (or Triple) Overhand Knot, as shown in the diagrams. The knot is then pulled up as tightly or loosely as is necessary for a good grip or as a free sliding noose.

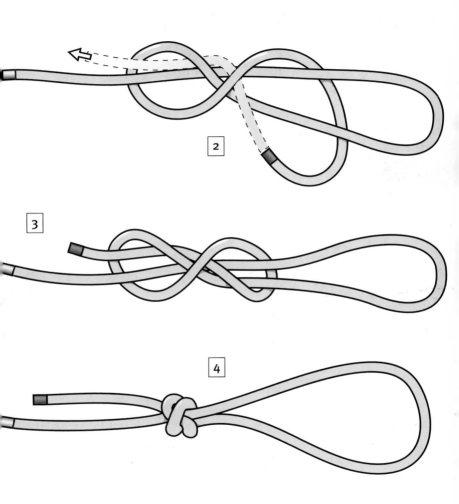

Fisherman's Loop *Also known as Englishman's Loop*

The Fisherman's Loop, or Englishman's Loop as it is sometimes known, was a much favored angler's loop for use with gut—but it works quite well with modern monofilament and other lines too.

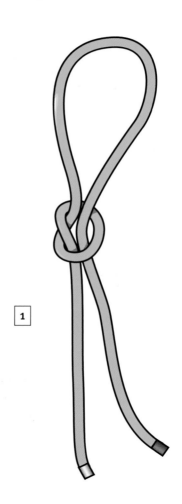

1

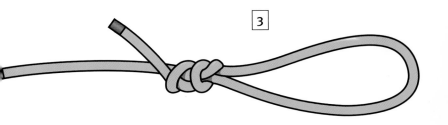

It is simply tied with two Overhand Knots as follows: tie a slipped Overhand Knot near the end of the line, adjust the loop to size, note or mark where the working end emerges from the knot, then put an Overhand Knot in the working end at that point before pulling the loop back to its full size.

Swami Loop *Also known as One-and-a-Half Fisherman's Loop*

Also known as the One-and-a-Half
Fisherman's Loop, the Swami Loop is an
adjustable loop that is as much at home
in monofilament fishing line as it is in a
climber's rope. Like the Fisherman's Loop
it provides an adjustable loop, but the
Double Overhand, instead of the
Overhand Knot, gives it that much more
security.

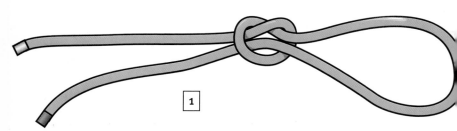

1

2

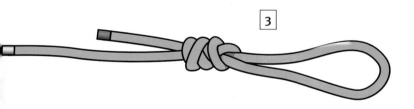

3

Make a slipped Overhand Knot near the end of the line, adjust the loop to the required size and mark the working end at the base of the knot. Now form a Double Overhand Knot, with the working end, using the grapevine method, over the standing part. When used to secure a rope to a ring, start with an Overhand Knot, pass the working end through the ring and back through the Overhand Knot (to form a Slipped Overhand Knot), then proceed as above.

Bowline (Common & Climber's)

There are at least five ways to tie the Common Bowline, three of which (the sailor's method, the one handed method and the line under tension), are not suited to learning from a book, as they require a certain amount of dexterity to achieve the correct result and this can only be assured by personal tuition. This leaves the method shown on pages 52–53 and the method shown here, which is accredited to climbers, but is ideal in many other situations.

Starting once again with that now familiar Slipped Overhand Knot (but leave it fairly open, otherwise the knot will not capsize in the later stages), the working end can now either be formed into a loop, or passed around an object. Now tuck the working end through the noose in the direction shown. It is worth noting that the working end is passed from the same side on which the collar is formed by the overhand knot around the noose, otherwise the working end will lie outside the Bowline's loop.

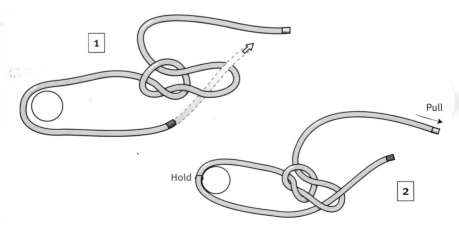

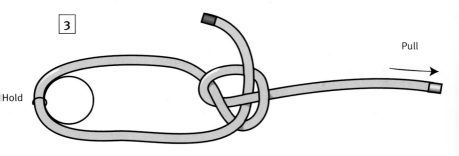

The next stage is to capsize the knot to form the Bowline—this is done either by laying back on the standing part, if the loop is around an object, or by holding the loop and pulling the standing part. When the knot is fully pulled up it will result in a Bowline. The finishing touch is to put either one or two Half Hitches in the working end around the loop to give it added security.

Water Bowline

Yet another useful Bowline, especially if you know it is going to bear a very heavy load that makes a Common Bowline difficult to untie, is the Water Bowline. Originally designed for use in man-made fiber ropes that were subjected to use in water (making the rope shrink and the Common Bowline difficult to untie), this knot has an added turn, which takes the majority of the load, leaving the first loop to hold the knot in place.

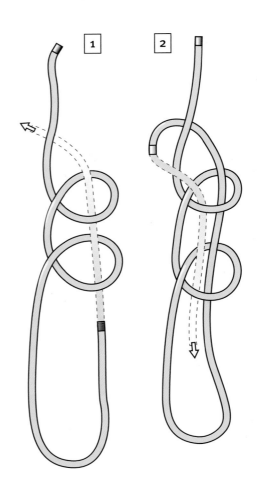

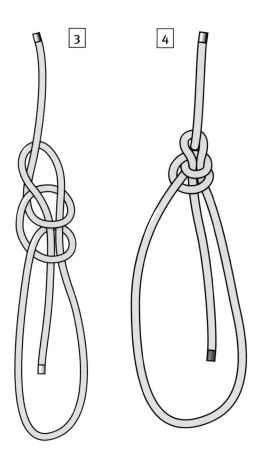

Make two crossing loops, as shown in the diagram (remember they should be shaped like a figure 6), then pass the working end up through both loops, around the back of the standing part and down through both loops again. Adjust the main loop to the required size and tighten the knot by pulling on the loop and the standing part.

Tucked Bowline

A favorite with tree climbers as a "tie in," the Tucked Bowline, or Bowline with the Yosemite Tie Off, is another way of both securing the knot to make it safer and to take the working end out of the loop, up alongside the standing part, where it can be taped or tied off with an Overhand or Double Overhand Knot.

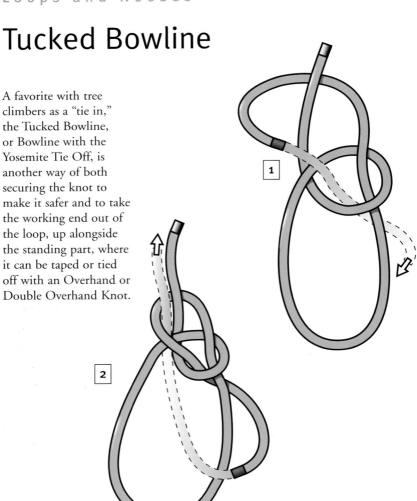

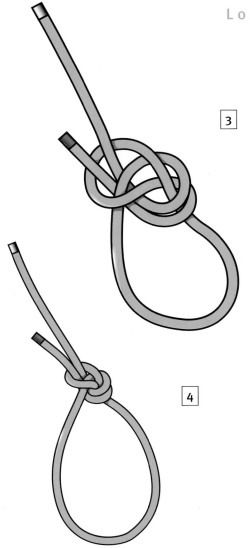

3

4

Tie a Common Bowline, but before pulling it up take the working end and pass it from behind the loop round in the same direction as the original crossed loop and up alongside it and the standing part as shown in diagrams 1 and 2. Dress the knot and pull it up by holding the standing part and the working end together and pulling down on the main loop.

Bowline on a Bight

The Bowline on a Bight is used when two loops are required that can be loaded together or separately. When under load the knot will be secure, but before it is loaded the loops can also be adjusted to different sizes.

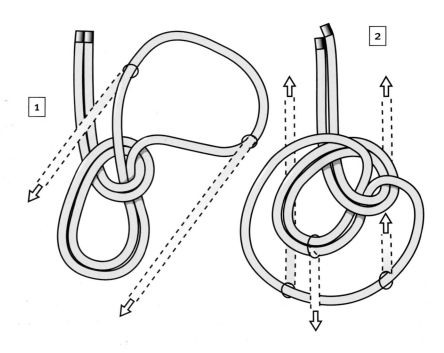

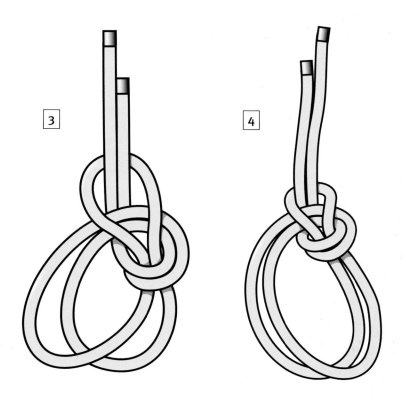

Make a long bight in the rope and commence the knot as you would a Common Bowline, but using the doubled rope as if it were one. Pass the end of the bight up through the crossing loop and open it out into a closed loop, large enough to pass over the twin main loops. Bring the closed loop down over the knot and up behind the twin loops, before holding and pulling down on the twin loops. Adjust the loop sizes and, holding the standing parts, pull down on the two loops to draw the knot up tight.

Running Bowline

If a loose noose is required, the Running Bowline is perhaps the most suited and easily tied. It can be formed either by tying a Common Bowline with a small loop and passing a bight of the standing part through the loop, or, if that is not practical, by tying it as shown here.

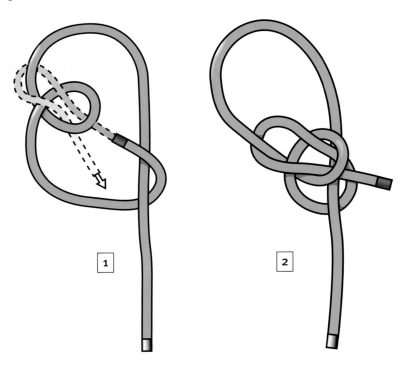

1

2

Start by forming a crossing loop and passing the working end around the standing part. Pass the working end through the crossing loop and round the back of the standing part, before completing the Bowline by passing it down through that loop.

Adjust the main loop (which is around the standing part), to suit and then hold the standing part and working end together and pull down on the loop.

3

Portuguese Bowline

The Portuguese Bowline provides two easily adjustable
loops. Use this knot only around inanimate objects, never
around a living body, because the two loops are in fact
one loop doubled and, even when loaded, if one loop is
extended the other will contract.

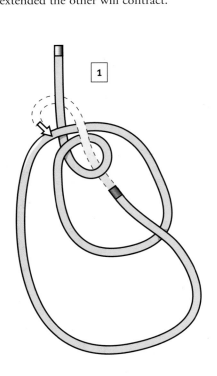

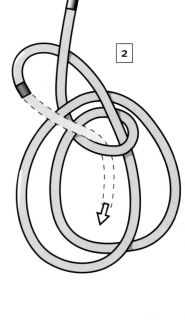

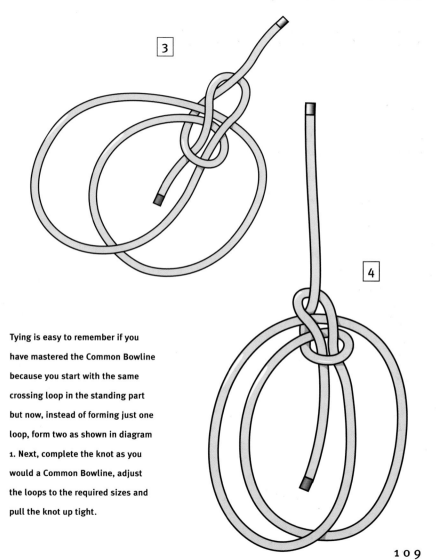

3

4

Tying is easy to remember if you have mastered the Common Bowline because you start with the same crossing loop in the standing part but now, instead of forming just one loop, form two as shown in diagram 1. Next, complete the knot as you would a Common Bowline, adjust the loops to the required sizes and pull the knot up tight.

Spanish Bowline

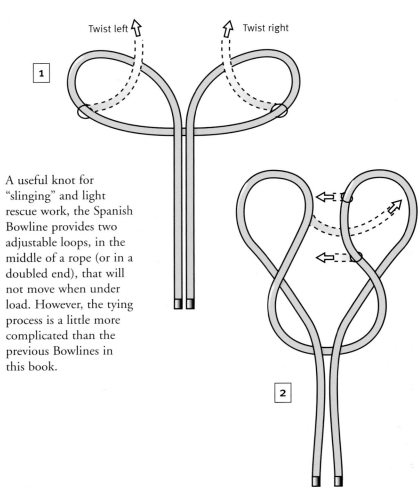

A useful knot for "slinging" and light rescue work, the Spanish Bowline provides two adjustable loops, in the middle of a rope (or in a doubled end), that will not move when under load. However, the tying process is a little more complicated than the previous Bowlines in this book.

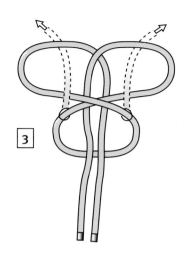

3

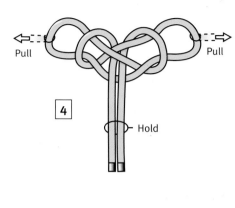

4

Pull

Pull

Hold

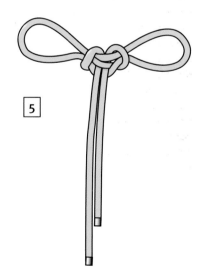

5

Start by taking a large bight in the rope and laying it out as shown in diagram 1. Twist the left-hand loop to the left and the right-hand loop to the right so that you end up with the two crossing loops shown in diagram 2. Pass the left loop through the right one as indicated in diagram 2, at the same time moving the right loop into the position that the left had occupied. Pull the lower two loops up through the upper loops, from front to back, as shown in diagram 3, before adjusting the knot and loop lengths and pulling the knot up tight by holding the standing parts and pulling on both "ears."

Handcuff Knot *Also known as Fireman's Chair Knot*

The Handcuff Knot, as its name implies, can (with care) be used as a wrist or ankle restraint; however it is much more likely to be used as an animal hobble, as a curtain holdback, or by placing the loops over both handles of a door, to stop it from shutting on tiny fingers. It can also be used in an emergency (but only when a proper harness is not available) as a Fireman's Chair Knot to hoist or lower a person; by adjusting the loops to be large enough to support the legs (behind the knees) and the torso (under the arms).

Form two crossing loops as shown in diagram 1, then pull them through each other as shown. Pull the knot up tight and adjust the loops to size—this is now a Handcuff Knot and the ends can be pulled up to reduce the size of the loops and secured with a Reef Knot. Alternatively, the ends can be Half Hitched over the loops (as shown in diagram 3) to secure them in a fixed position—resulting in the Fireman's Chair Knot as shown in diagram 4.

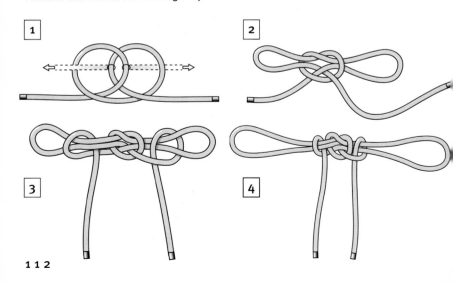

Tom Fool Knot

Another start to either of these knots is the Tom Fool Knot—it is perhaps not so efficient as a Handcuff Knot, but does equally well as the Fireman's Chair. The difference is that the two loops are made in such a way that, when formed, the two leads are on the outside, as shown in the diagram.

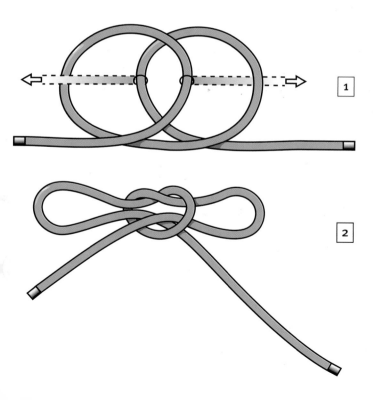

Alpine Butterfly Loop

The Alpine Butterfly Loop, or Lineman's Loop as it is sometimes called, is a favorite of climbers because it is easily tied, can be loaded in all directions and is easy to inspect during a safety check. Essentially it forms attaching points in a rope that can be used for karabiners, hooks or even other ropes.

There are two commonly used methods of tying this knot. The first is to take a bight in the rope and twist a crossing turn into it, following this with another twist in the same direction, so forming two loops as in diagram 1.

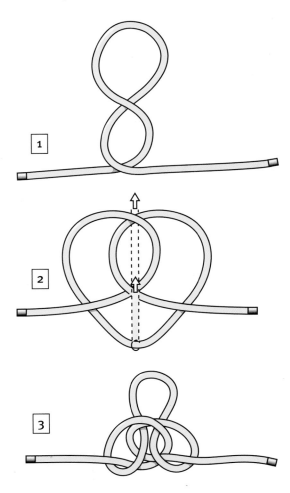

Now bring the top of the upper loop down behind the knot to form what looks like a heart shape, before continuing with the top of the loop through the lower loop from front to back.

Adjust the loop to size and pull the knot up by heaving on the two ends. The second method is to make three turns around the hand or arm, take the top of the left hand turn and move it to the center (diagram 4); now take the new left hand turn and move it to the right over the other two, before passing it back under those two loops to the left. Hold the loop and pull up on the two ends.

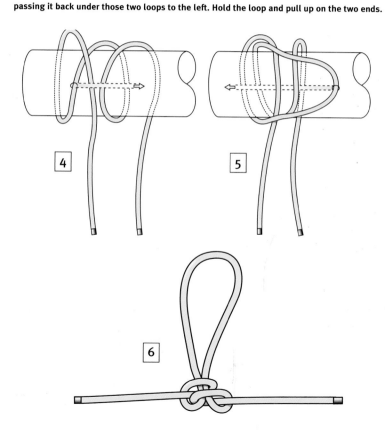

Blood Loop Dropper Knot

Also known as a Dropper Loop, the Blood Loop Dropper Knot is used mainly by fishermen to form an attachment point in a paternoster on which they can suspend "droppers," the lines that hold their hooks.

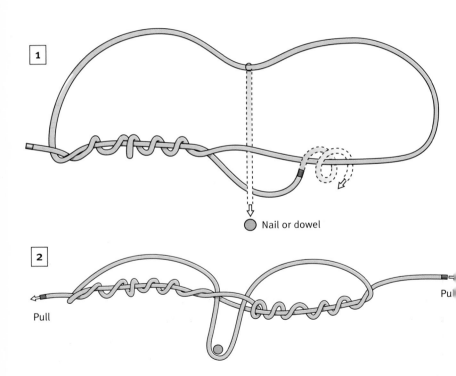

1

Nail or dowel

2

Pull

Pull

116

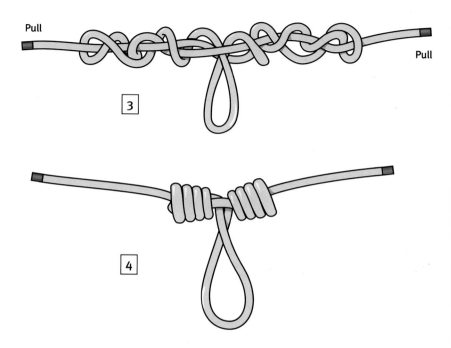

Pull

Pull

3

4

It is tied in a length of monofilament of which both ends need to be available. First tie an Overhand Knot to form a large loop, then twist one end to the left as shown in the diagram, and the other to the right, using at least four turns in each end—the loop belly needs to be at least the width of the turns because it will need to spiral over the turns to form the knot. When both sets of turns are complete, pass the center of the belly loop through the center of the turns as shown here—it helps if you use a fixed hook, nail or dowel to hold this while you pull on both ends to tighten up the knot. Lubricate the knot with saliva or water, then pull in the direction shown in diagram 2; the knot should be pulling up as shown in diagram 3.

Lanyard Loop Knot

Also known as Bosun's Whistle Knot

Sometimes called the Bosun's Whistle Knot, the Lanyard Loop Knot is in construction also a Diamond Knot, which in turn can be formed into a Chinese Button Knot. This is both a functional and a decorative knot that can be used to make a loop for a whistle lanyard, a zipper pull, a key fob, and many other useful items.

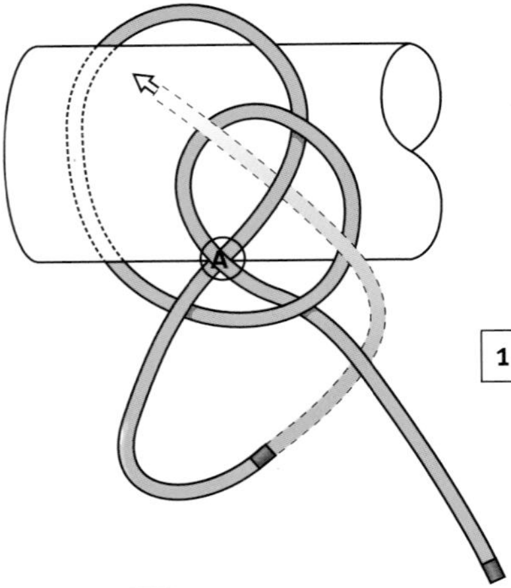

1

2

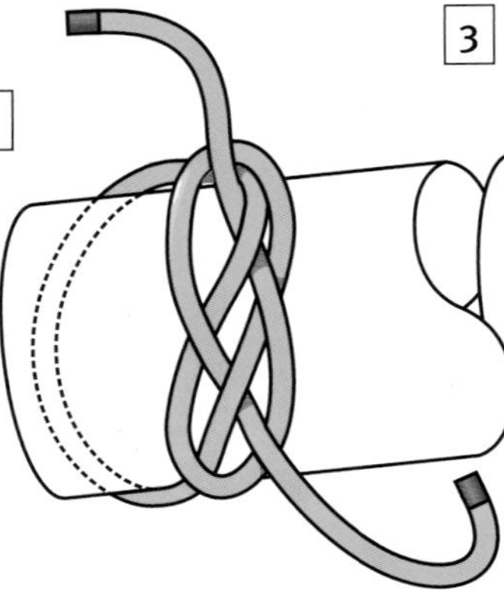

3

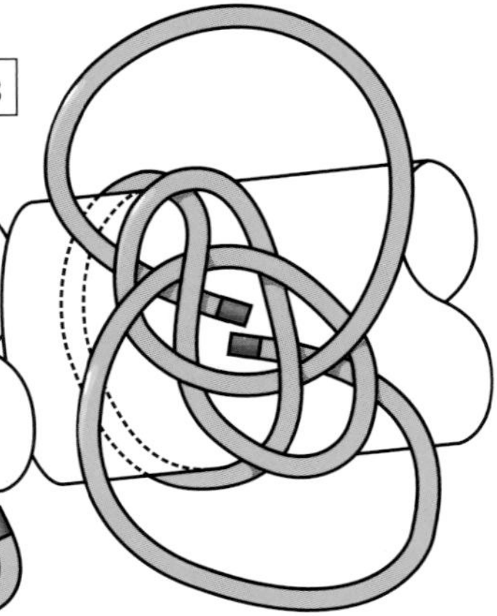

Begin tying by passing a turn around the hand or a
cardboard tube—take the lead that is at the back to the right
behind the lead in the front, and form a crossing loop over the
front lead and hold it at mark A in diagram 1. You will find that if
you put a right twist in the line with your thumb and index finger, the
loop will form easily. You should now take the front lead and pass it
behind the working end of the crossing loop and up through the
knot in an "over, under, over" sequence until it emerges from the
knot at the top left. You should now have a knot that resembles a
Carrick Bend with a loop at the back, as shown in diagram 2. Take the
upper lead emerging from the left down beside the
knot, around the back loop where it emerges from the
knot and into the center aperture in the Carrick Bend.
Then take the lower right-hand lead and pass it up
beside the knot, around the back loop where it joins the
knot and again into the center aperture of the Carrick Bend—
pull these two up through the center and out of the knot. Slide the
arrangement off the hand or tube, then, holding the loop, gently pull
both ends at the same time until the knot starts to form as in diagram 4.
Pull the knot up tight by working round the knot and gradually (do not pull
it too tight on the first round) tightening it up. To make a Chinese Button
Knot—instead of maintaining a loop draw it into the knot and put a couple of
needle and cotton stitches in it to hold it in place.

4

5

Sliding Double Fisherman's Loop

The Sliding Double Fisherman's Loop has both practical and decorative applications. It forms a versatile double loop that can be adjusted fairly easily to suit various sling applications in the climbing world as well as being suited to indoor décor as a curtain holdback or anti-slam device on a door.

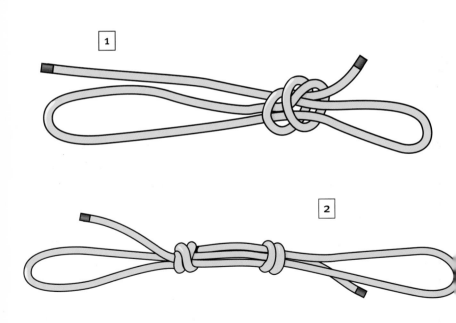

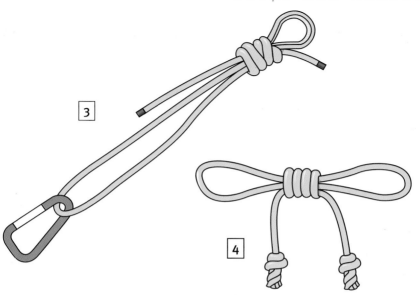

Form a long loop with generous working ends, then proceed to tie a pair of Double Overhand Knots (using the grapevine method) over the loop as shown in diagram 1. Pull the knots up fairly tight and slide them together as you would for a Fisherman's Knot. You now have two loops that you can adjust to suit your requirement.

The first completed knot (diagram 3) shows how a hard eye, of suitable size, can be inserted in one of the loops, and it will hold well provided the Double Overhand Knots are pulled up tight.

The second completed knot (diagram 4) shows how this same arrangement, with a little adornment (Double Overhand Knot with the ends teased out) on the ends of the line, can make a very attractive curtain holdback.

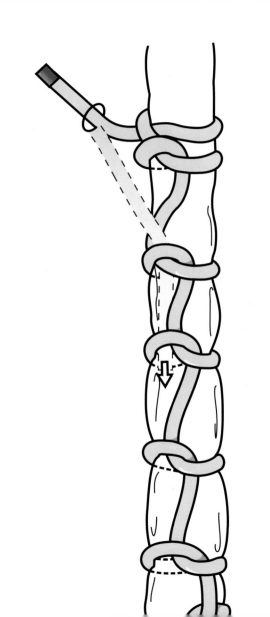

Knots for Binding and Holding

Introduction

In this section, we look at a selection of knots that cover the needs of everyday life and adventurous pursuits.

Starting with some simple knots that we use in our everyday tasks, like the Reef Knot, we then progress to some interesting knots that provide a stranglehold on ropes, bags, packages, sacks and other items that we use from day to day. There are knots to support and secure loads to a truck, trailer, wagon, roof rack, or deck, as well as those knots we use to bundle up items, or lash to a fixture to make them safe or to stop damage. Finally we look at the lashings for tying together anything from small garden canes to larger poles for pioneering projects, including a little-known method of making something like a tree house floor, by lashing poles together.

List of Knots and Uses

GENERAL PURPOSE

REEF KNOT—Tie the ends of a rope or bandage together. **Page 126**

THIEF KNOT—Novelty knot only. **Page 126**

SURGEON'S KNOT—Tie the ends of slippery material together. **Page 127**

CONSTRICTOR KNOT—Make a temporary Whipping. **Page 128**

DOUBLE CONSTRICTOR KNOT—Tie a line around a cylindrical object, which when tied will grip and hold. **Page 128**

BAG KNOT—Tie off the top of a sack or bag. **Page 129**

STRANGLE KNOT—Tie off the top of a sack or jar cover. **Page 129**

PACKER'S KNOT—Tie string around a parcel or joint of meat. **Page 130**

FLAT SEIZING—Bind two parts of a rope together to form an eye. **Page 138**

CAMPING & CLIMBING

OKLAHOMA HITCH—Wrap a bundle of sticks or poles together, or suspend a scaffold plank. **Page 132**

TRUCKER'S HITCH—Tie down a load over a trailer, truck, roof rack, etc. **Page 134**

TRANSOM KNOT—Tie bamboo canes or sticks together at right angles. **Page 139**

SNAKE OR RAFT LASHING—Make a floor with sticks or poles. **Page 140**

FILIPINO LASHING—Lash two poles together at right angles. **Page 142**

SQUARE LASHING—Lash two poles together at right angles. **Page 144**

SHEAR LASHING—Lash two poles to form an "A frame" or "Sheerlegs." **Page 146**

DIAGONAL LASHING—Secure cross poles on a pole frame. **Page 148**

BOATING

LASHING (MARLIN HITCHING)—Lash up a hammock or sail to a boom. **Page 136**

LASHING (CHAIN HITCHING)—Lash a bundle that can be released quickly. **Page 137**

Half Knot Binding Knots

This series of Half Knots is here for completeness, as they also appear in a previous section. Diagram 1 is the Reef Knot or Square Knot (page 37), which is a knot that lies flat, making it particularly suitable for tying bandages.

Diagram 2 is the Thief Knot, which is more of a novelty than a useful knot (compare where the ends emerge from the knot with the Square Knot). It is said that sailors tied their kit bags with this knot to detect if it had been untied because the unsuspecting intruder would almost certainly replace it with a Square Knot!

Diagram 3 is the Slipped Overhand Knot (page 38), which is useful if you need the function of a Square Knot, but want one that is quick and easy to untie, like a duffle bag drawstring, for example.

Then there is the Surgeon's Knot (diagram 4); the added tuck in the first Overhand gives this stage a little more holding power while you tie the second one—especially useful when using slippery cord.

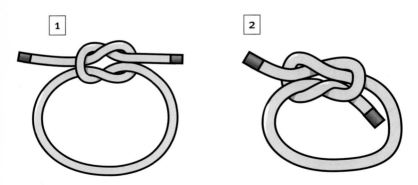

3

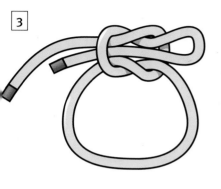

To tie: diagram 1—Right over left, tuck and pull—left over right, tuck and tie.

diagram 2—Make a bight in one end of the line, pass the other end up through the bight on the side of the other working end, round the two legs of the bight and back down through the bight.

diagram 3—Right over left, tuck and pull—left over right and pull through a bight.

diagram 4 - Right over left, make two tucks and pull—left over right, tuck and tie.

4

Constrictor Knots

You will have met the Constrictor Knot (page 58) already, but there are some similar knots that have been used over the years to tie bags and bundles.

Diagram 1 is a reminder of the Constrictor Knot, while diagram 2 is a Double Constrictor Knot that is particularly useful as a temporary whipping or for use on slippery ropes.

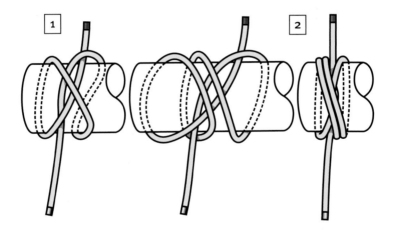

The Double Constrictor Knot (shown in diagram 2) is tied as follows — Make a crossing turn on the object, bring the working end round and make a second crossing turn, then up to the left of the standing part before tucking the end under it.

Bag and Strangle Knots

The Bag Knot (diagram 3) is also known as a Miller's Knot, as it was once used to tie off the tops of flour sacks.

The Strangle Knot (diagram 4) looks very much like the Constrictor Knot, but note how the crossover lies 'in' the Overhand Knot, and not across it—thus it is less secure and easier to untie.

To tie the Bag Knot (diagram 3), pass a bight over the bag neck, cross the two ends (right over left), then take the working end round the bag once and tuck it under the standing part, as shown in the diagram. Pull both ends to tighten.

The Strangle Knot (diagram 4) is started like the Bag Knot, but the working end is crossed over the standing part, then tucked under it to form a Half Knot under the crossing turn, as shown. Pull up using both ends.

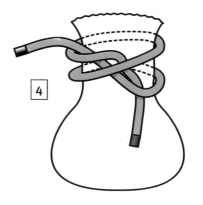

129

Packer's Knot *Also known as Butcher's Knot*

The Packer's Knot, or Butcher's Knot, is used to start binding a parcel or a rolled joint of meat, and for many other applications where a stranglehold is needed while you tie the knot off (diagram 3), or make more turns or hitches around the object.

In the kitchen, it can also be used to tie down cloths and paper over pudding basins, or to hold the brown paper around a cake baking tin.

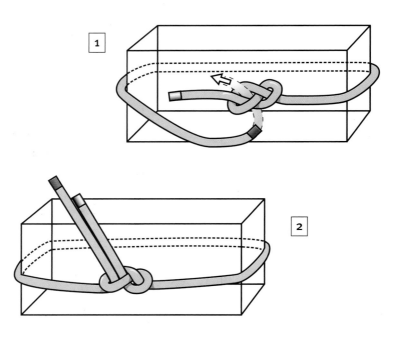

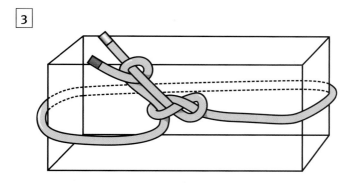

3

Tie a Figure of Eight Knot in one end, leaving a tail long enough to be able to hold it and to tie off on if necessary. Pass the working end around the object, then through the knot in the same direction as the tail, as shown in diagram 1. Pull up the tail, to tighten the Figure of Eight Knot, then pull on the working end to tighten the noose around the object.

To secure it in position, tie one or two Half Hitches, with the working end, around the tail. To untie, release the Half Hitches and pull on the tail.

Oklahoma Hitch

Also known as the Scaffold Hitch, the Oklahoma Hitch can be used to suspend a plank of wood at each end, or it is equally effective for gathering and tying a bundle of sticks, poles, pipes or similar items together.

Because the tension on this binding is easily adjusted, it is also suitable in First Aid situations, to tie around emergency splints on a fractured limb.

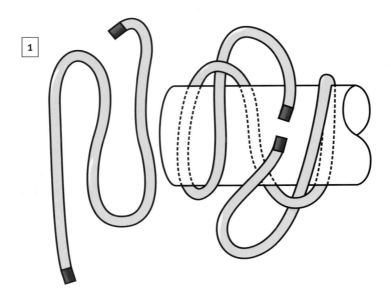

1

2

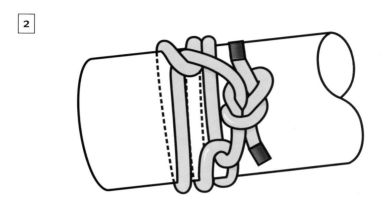

Lay a bight of the rope, line or a bandage in a Z shape on the ground—lay the plank or bundle items

on top of this. Now take the ends and pass each of them down through its corresponding bight in the

Z. Bring the two ends together, pulling them both at the same time, as tight as is necessary, then tie

off—using a Bowline to suspend a plank, or a Reef Knot if tying a bundle.

Trucker's Hitch *Also known as Wagoner's Hitch*

Often called the Trucker's Dolly, or Wagoner's Hitch, the Trucker's Hitch is still much used, despite the availability of ratchet tie-down devices. The reason this knot is so popular is that it works rather like a block and tackle and can exert considerable force on the load. Apart from tying loads down on a truck, trailer, roof rack or similar, it can also be used as a tent guy line, or storm lashing tightening device or even an overhead lifting/lowering device for light loads.

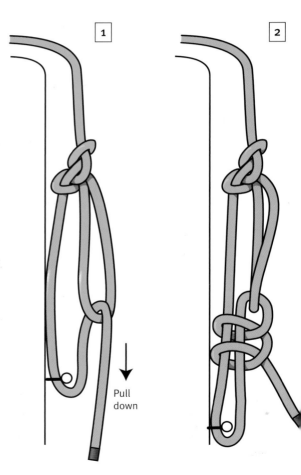

1

Pull down

2

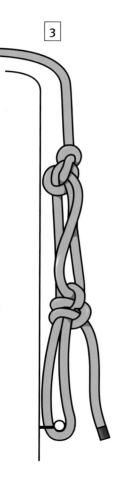

The conventional method of tying the Trucker's Hitch is to start with the Bellringer's Hitch (page 36), but without a load on it, as when loading slippery line like Polypropylene the hitch can very easily fall apart. In reality, any suitable loop can be used; the Slipped Overhand, the Manharness Hitch or the Alpine Butterfly are perhaps the most suitable. In this example, the Alpine Butterfly Loop is used. Secure the line to one side of the load with a secure hitch like a Round Turn and Two Half Hitches or Anchor Bend. At a point, as high as you can reach up to, tie a suitable loop—the Alpine Butterfly is tied by making three turns around the hand, then bringing the left turn into the center; next, bring the new left turn towards the finger tips, then back under all the turns towards the wrist, before pulling the two ends to tighten it. Now pass the working end down under a securing bar or round a hook on the vehicle, and up through the loop, as shown in diagram 1, then bear down on the working end to tighten, as shown in diagram 2. Secure with Two Half Hitches close to the bottom of the loop as shown in diagram 3.

Lashing (Marlin Hitching)

Traditionally used by sailors to lash up their hammocks (with left-hand laid three strand rope), Marlin Hitching still has its uses today for lashing together any long bundle into a nice tight wrap.

Form an eye in one end of the line, using either an Eye Splice, Timber Hitch or Overhand Loop. Pass the working end around the bundle and through the eye. Now coil the line and hold it in the right hand, pass it over the bundle and transfer it to the left hand underneath it (or vice versa if you are left handed), then pass it over and under the standing part to form what looks like a Half Knot. Transfer back to the right hand and pull down on the right side to draw the knot up tight, then "lay back" on the line to bring it tighter and lay it along the bundle. Repeat as many times as necessary, then finish with Two Half Hitches (Clove Hitch), and tuck any end that is left back along the top, to make a tidy finish.

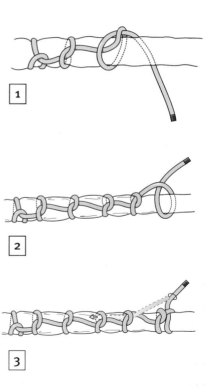

Lashing (Chain Hitching)

Chain Hitching is very quick to apply and even quicker to untie. Use it to temporarily lash a sail to a boom to stop it flailing about, or to tie back a tarpaulin that may be needed in a hurry.

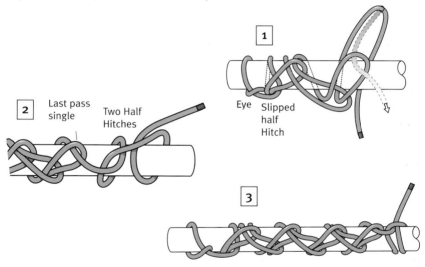

1

Eye Slipped half Hitch

2 Last pass single Two Half Hitches

3

Start with a Timber Hitch around both the pole and the item to be lashed. Now, pass the line from left to right around the objects, but instead of pulling the end through, pull through a bight—thus forming a Slipped Half Hitch. Put your hand through the loop and to the right of the objects and pick up a bight of the line and pull it through and along the top of the lashing. Put your hand through the last loop down to the left of the objects and pull another bight through and along the center line. Repeat as many times as necessary, alternating left and right, then pull the end through the last loop. Finish with Two Half Hitches (Clove Hitch). To release the lashing, untie the Clove Hitch, pull the end through the last loop, then pull the line, and it will all come undone like a zip.

Flat Seizing

The Flat Seizing is used primarily to bind one piece of rope parallel to another, perhaps to form an eye, in the end of a rope or particularly in a bight where an eye splice is not possible. It is ideal for inserting a hard eye into the bight of a rope to be used at the head of a rope ladder or swing ropes.

The Seizing should be done using a strong whipping twine, of a thickness that will not cut into the rope fibers, yet is fine enough to have a good grip. Start by forming an eye in the end of the twine, then pass the working end through it and pull up taut, keeping the eye over the center of the two ropes. Commence laying on the turns around both ropes—each turn needs to be VERY tight, so it is wise to wear a leather glove or use a metal rod and Marlin Hitch when pulling them up. Lay on enough turns to cover the length equal to about two diameters of the rope. Next, pass the twine between the ropes, then under the turns and back through the eye, then round between the ropes and over the turns, forming "Frapping Turns," which must also be very tight. Finish by putting Two Half Hitches around the Frapping Turns, then loose the end up under the seizing.

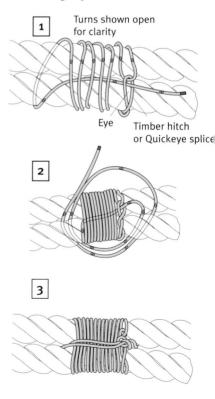

Turns shown open for clarity

Eye   Timber hitch or Quickeye splice

Transom Knot

The Transom Knot is a very useful variant of the Constrictor Knot that will lash two small sticks or garden canes together to form a cross. It can also be used as a temporary Square Lashing when laying out pioneering projects, before they are lashed properly.

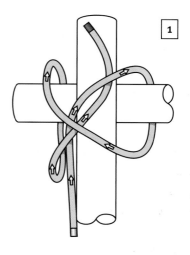

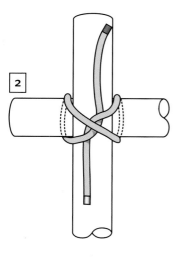

Lay the two canes as shown in diagram 1 — pass the line over the vertical cane and down to the right under the horizontal cane. Bring it up, over itself and down to the left and under the horizontal cane. Now bring the end up, over the standing part, under itself then under the standing part, as shown, pull tight and cut off the ends (which can be cut fairly close to the knot).

Snake or Raft Lashing

Here is an application where the Transom Knot is safer and more versatile than conventional Snake Lashing. Whether making a floor for a tree house, a raft of logs, or just a little shelf with sticks for use by the camp fire or ablutions, tying the boards to the beams, so to speak, is less frustrating when you can secure each one as you lay it on.

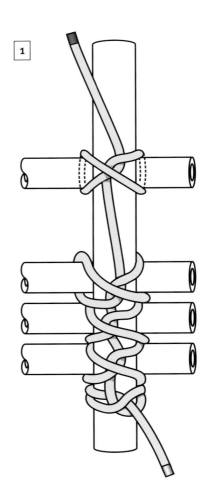

1

In diagram 2 the vertical pole is the beam, the horizontal pole the first board. Start tying by putting a Clove Hitch on the beam, and note that all the knotting will lie along the beam—both for security and for a neat finish on the top.

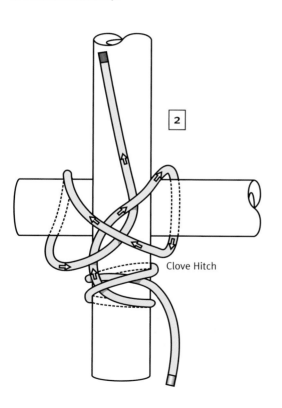

2

Clove Hitch

Pass the line down to the right, under the board and back up across the beam and itself. Now pass it down to the left under the board and back up across the standing part, under itself and under the standing part again. Pull this knot up as tight as possible.

Lay the next board to be lashed, either up close to the first, or (here is where the advantage of this method comes in—each board is held by an individual knot) a suitable distance from it, before applying the next Transom Knot. Complete with a Clove Hitch around the beam.

Filipino Lashing

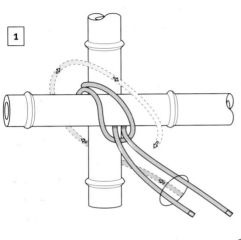

The Filipino Lashing is ideal for lashing together bamboo canes or poles to make garden trelliswork or plant tepee structures. It is quick and easy to tie (as well as to remember) and needs only a Square Knot to secure it.

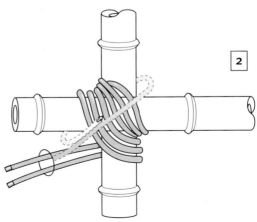

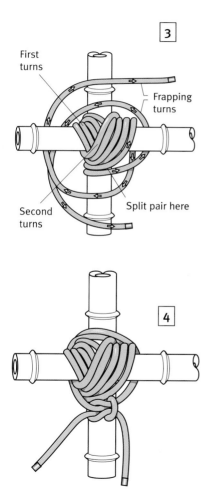

First turns

Frapping turns

Second turns

Split pair here

First position the canes—if you are building a large structure use Transom Knots to hold the canes in place. Middle a piece of garden twine, then tie a Lark's Head Knot diagonally across the two canes, as shown in diagram 1. Keeping the two lines together, pass them around the vertical cane and back in the direction shown. Make two or three turns, then change direction by 90 degrees and make two or three turns diagonally across the top of the first turns. Split the pair in front of the vertical cane, take one in front over the horizontal cane and one behind it as shown in diagram 3. Pass at least two frapping turns in each direction as tightly as you can around the diagonal turns, before tying off with a Square Knot.

Square Lashing

A Square Lashing is put on two poles to lash them together at or near to right angles to each other. The term "square" indicates that the lashing turns are put on square with the poles. Used primarily in pioneering projects, it is much stronger, more reliable and better suited to large poles and rope than the Filipino Lashing.

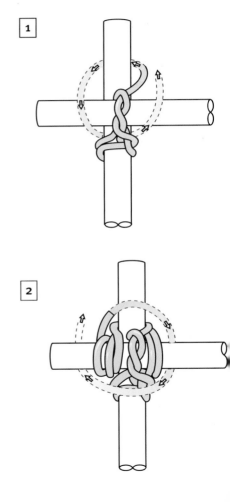

Lay the poles to be lashed, at or near to right angles to each other, the upper one being the horizontal pole. Tie a Clove Hitch on the vertical pole, just below where you want the horizontal one to rest, leaving an end long enough to take a few turns around the standing part, as shown in diagram 1. Pass the working end over the horizontal pole to the right, round behind the vertical and back to the front. Now go round the back of the vertical pole on top of the

Clove Hitch, then back to the front of the horizontal and outside of the first turn. Pull this first pass up as tight as you can, then repeat the sequence above for at least three turns, remembering to pass the lead inside the back turns on the vertical pole (see diagram 4) and outside the front turns on the horizontal pole, heaving each turn up as tight as you can. After the last pass, apply at least two frapping turns as shown in diagram 3, to bring the knot up really tight, before tying the working end off with Two Half Hitches (Clove Hitch), with the lead into the first one being as close to the finish of the frapping turns as possible.

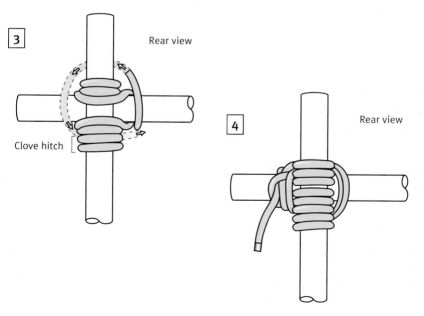

3

Rear view

Clove hitch

4

Rear view

Shear Lashing

There are two main functions of Shear Lashing; one is to lash together two poles to form "Shear Legs," the other to lash two (or more) poles together to extend their length—for which you will need to apply at least two lashings.

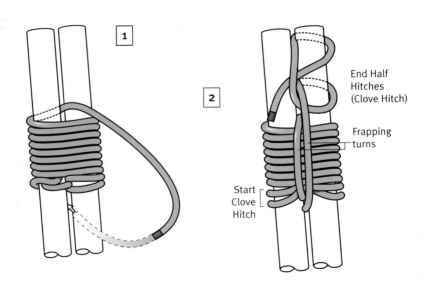

1

2

End Half
Hitches
(Clove Hitch)

Frapping
turns

Start
Clove
Hitch

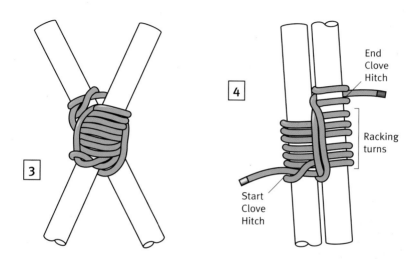

To make Shear Legs—start by tying a Clove Hitch around one pole (leaving sufficient end to twist around the working part of the rope). Take the working end and make eight or ten turns, no more than hand tight, around both poles as shown in diagram 1. Now apply a couple of frapping turns as shown in diagram 2, before tying off with Two Half Hitches (Clove Hitch), around the opposite pole to the one you started on. Note: there are other options for tying this lashing, e.g. finishing with a Clove Hitch around both poles, but that method originated in the age of natural fiber ropes—slippery nylon or Polythene ropes will not hold as well.

To lash two poles together to extend their length, as shown in diagram 4— again, this method is not "conventional" but works better with slippery ropes. Make a Clove Hitch around the lower pole, and then apply at least eight Racking Turns (see Racking Bend) as tightly as possible around both poles. Apply a couple of frapping turns and tie off with a Clove Hitch around the upper pole.

Diagonal Lashing

Diagonal Lashing, as its name implies, is applied diagonally across the axis of the poles being lashed together. This lashing is normally used to attach diagonal cross members to frames and so the angles between each of the poles can vary quite a bit, making Square Lashing unsuitable.

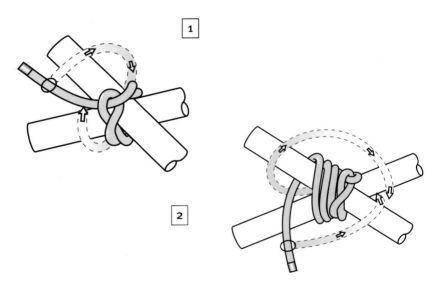

Begin by applying a Timber Hitch diagonally across the two poles, in the space with the largest angle between the poles, as in diagram 1. Follow the Timber Hitch round at least three times, then change direction to make the same number of turns at right angles to the first ones. Pull each turn up as tightly as possible.

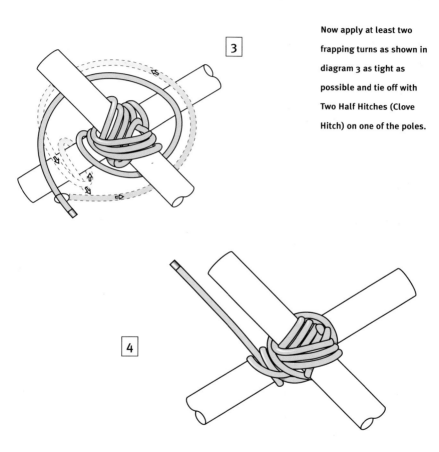

3

Now apply at least two frapping turns as shown in diagram 3 as tight as possible and tie off with Two Half Hitches (Clove Hitch) on one of the poles.

4

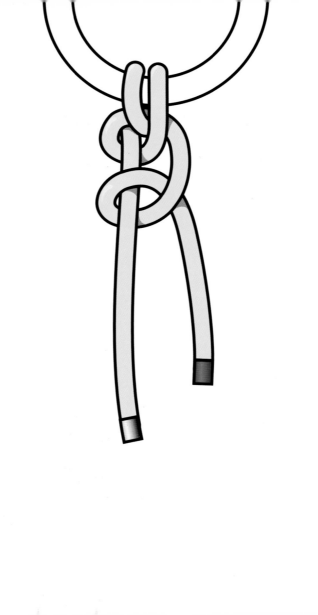

Knots Used to Attach Ropes and Lines

Introduction

Whether it is tying up your dog or mooring an aircraft carrier, there comes a time when we all need to tie a rope, line, wire, or tape to something using knots. The series of knots we use to attach a rope to another object, be it a pole, post, ring, bollard, or even another rope, are called "Hitches." However, as in all things in life there are exceptions, and within this section there is a description of a knot called the "Anchor Bend," which is really a Hitch. This anomaly came about because the Anchor Bend is also known as a "Fisherman's Bend"—and there is also a Fisherman's Knot that is a true Bend.

We start with a few knots that you were introduced to in earlier sections, then move on to those hitches that are useful to boaters, travelers, tree climbers, lumberjacks, and many other occupations and pursuits. Two of particular note are the Icicle Hitch and Blake's Hitch, which are relatively new to the knotting scene. The first of these was demonstrated at an IGKT meeting by John Smith from Surrey, England, and is one of those knots that is not only very useful in a wide variety of situations, but also intriguing in its efficiency. The other is Blake's Hitch, shown to me by a tree climber—I have included it here in print because the only reference I can find to it, at the moment, is on the Internet.

List of Knots and Uses

Clove Hitches

As the Clove Hitch was learned in the section on Everyday Knots, these four variants are included in this section for completeness. The much used Clove Hitch to a rail or rope is shown in diagram 1, and its slipped version in diagram 2. Diagram 3 shows the Clove Hitch applied to a ring, with an added Half Hitch to make it more secure. Finally, diagram 4 is a reminder of how a Clove Hitch is applied to a post.

Please refer to the tying instructions on pages 44-46.

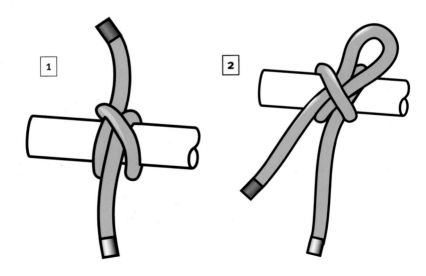

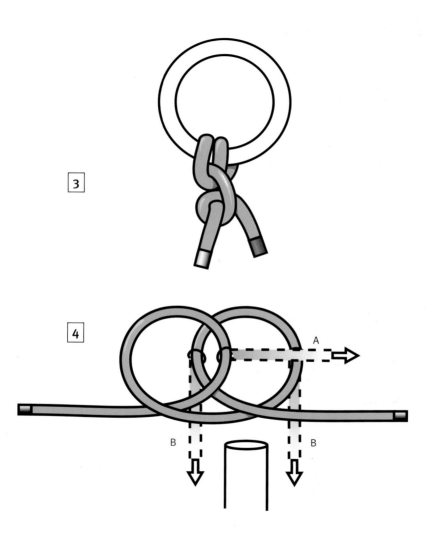

Cow Hitch and Variants

The Cow Hitch has a whole family of names, most depicting the use to which the knot is normally applied. The Cow Hitch is normally associated with the knot depicted in diagram 2 with the load being applied only to one side of the knot. If you did actually tether an animal to a peg like this, it would soon rotate the knot so much that the working end would slip through the knot and release it.

Dr. Harry Asher came up with the idea that prevents this and named it the Pedigree Cow Hitch, which is shown in diagram 3, while Clifford Ashley passed the end from the standing part side and refers to it as a "Snug Hitch."

The knot in diagram 4, tied so that both ends are used, is commonly known as a Lark's Head, especially in Macramé. Some other variants include the Ring Hitch (shown in diagram 5), Bale Sling Hitch, Running Hitch, and Label Hitch.

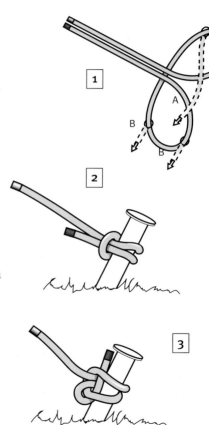

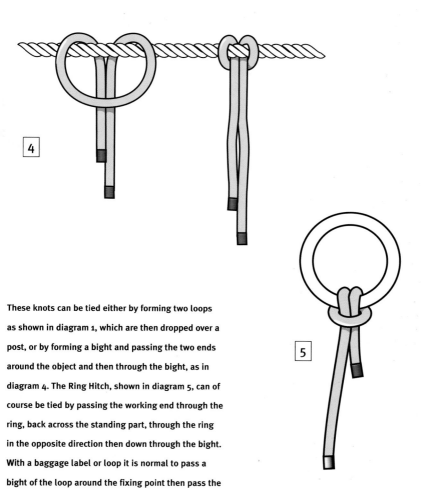

These knots can be tied either by forming two loops as shown in diagram 1, which are then dropped over a post, or by forming a bight and passing the two ends around the object and then through the bight, as in diagram 4. The Ring Hitch, shown in diagram 5, can of course be tied by passing the working end through the ring, back across the standing part, through the ring in the opposite direction then down through the bight. With a baggage label or loop it is normal to pass a bight of the loop around the fixing point then pass the label, or the opposite bight, through the first one.

Timber Hitch

The Timber Hitch makes a temporary noose that can be easily tied around the girth of a large log or other round object and quickly untied. However it must be remembered that this knot will only function and remain tied if there is a load on it. The principle behind this knot is that the end is twisted around its own part that is entrapped and held to itself by resting firmly against an object.

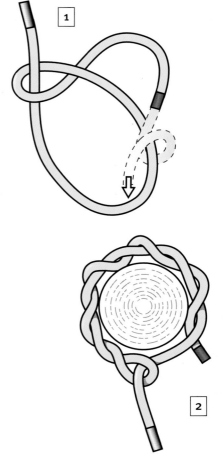

Pass the rope around the object, take the working end around the standing part and then twist it around itself as shown in diagram 1. If stranded rope is used, the working end should be twisted with the lay of the rope—i.e., with right hand laid rope the end is twisted to the right. Position the knot and pull on the standing part to tighten the noose around the object, maintaining a load.

Killick Hitch

A "killick" is an anchor, so quite naturally this knot originated from being used to make a makeshift anchor using a boulder or other heavy object. It is now more likely to be used to haul a log, plank, or other long object by one end either over the ground or in the water.

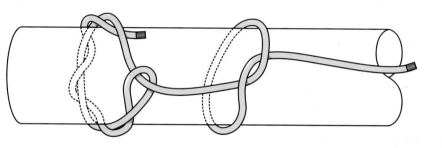

Tie a Timber Hitch around the object and then apply either a Half Hitch or a Marline Hitch a little further along the object and in the direction of the tow. The advantage of a Marline Hitch over the Half Hitch is that it will hold better if the tow goes slack.

Cat's Paw

The Cat's Paw is used to attach a rope sling, strop or the bight of a rope to a hook. The arrangement stops the sling from slipping over the hook, especially if the load is not balanced.

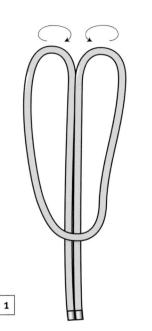

1

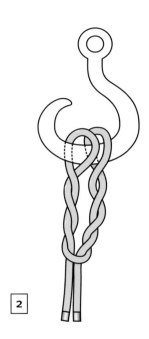

2

Pick up two bights from the rope or sling, about shoulder width apart, to form an arrangement like that shown in diagram 1. Now twist the two loops in opposite directions using at least three turns, put the two loops over the hook, dress the knot by pulling on the two ends, and it is ready to use.

Round Turn and Two Half Hitches

This knot is repeated here again to keep the section complete. Probably one of the most used and reliable knots, the Round Turn and Two Half Hitches is a combination of the Round Turn, which holds the load using friction between the rope and the rail, and two Half Hitches, which stop the turns from slipping. It is one of the primary knots in a sailor's repertoire and used either as a temporary or as a long term Hitch.

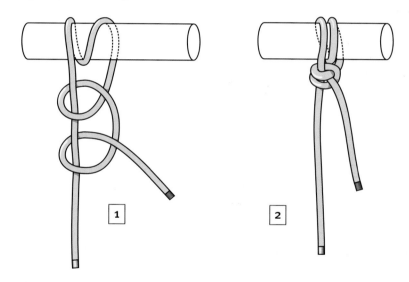

1

2

Pass the rope twice around the rail/ring/post, adjust the turns to hold the load, then apply two Half Hitches with the working end over the load-bearing standing part. If the knot is going to be subjected to a lot of movement it will be prudent to seize the working end to the standing part, using the Flat Seizing shown on page 138.

161

Rolling Hitch

Sometimes referred to as the Magnus Hitch, the Rolling Hitch is used to attach a rope to an object when a sideways pull is required. There are two common variations to this knot. The first, as shown in diagrams 1 to 3, has a double crossover and therefore a better grip and is used on poles and other smooth objects. The second is the more conventional method, shown in diagram 4, and is used to attach one rope to another—useful for taking the weight off one rope while transferring it to another fixing or when taking the riding turns off a winch drum. The Magnus Hitch or Taut-Line Hitch variation of this knot is covered on page 172.

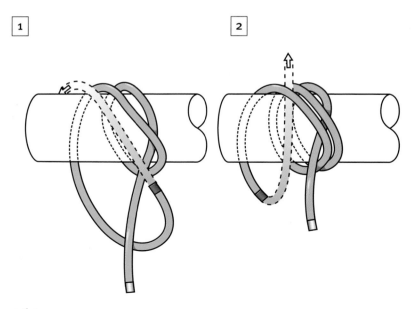

To tie around a pole with the direction of pull to the right—Pass a crossing turn around the pole, then go back to the right of the standing part and over it once more as in diagram 1. Secure with a Half Hitch as shown in diagram 2, pull the knot up tight using both ends, then apply the pull to the right. If the pull is to be to the left then the knot must be tied with the two crossing turns on the left of the standing part.

To secure a small rope to a larger one for a pull to the right—Make a round turn over the rope then bring the working end across the front of the standing part and secure with a Half Hitch, as shown in diagram 4.

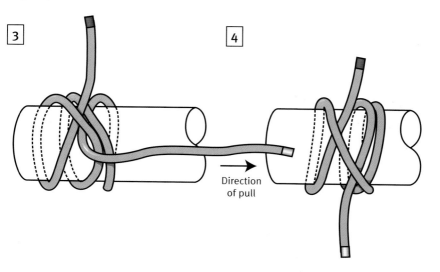

Direction of pull

Pile Hitch

Simple yet very effective, the Pile Hitch can be used for attaching a line to piles, stakes, posts, bollards, etc.

Apart from its nautical use for attaching berthing lines to piles and bollards, it is also useful as a boundary line fixed to stakes or pegs, as it will take a pull on both sides.

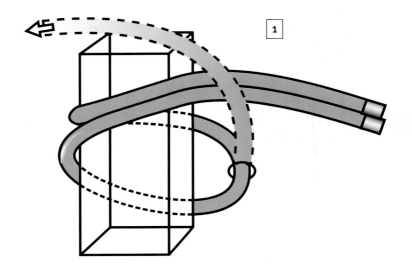

1

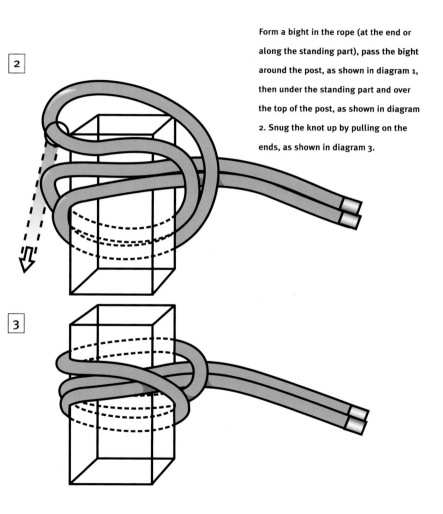

Form a bight in the rope (at the end or along the standing part), pass the bight around the post, as shown in diagram 1, then under the standing part and over the top of the post, as shown in diagram 2. Snug the knot up by pulling on the ends, as shown in diagram 3.

Icicle Hitch

The Icicle Hitch, devised by John Smith, is based on the Pile Hitch and although quite new to the knotting scene it is rapidly replacing the Rolling Hitch as a sideways pulling attachment. The grip that this knot achieves is quite remarkable even on smooth cylindrical surfaces. Pulled up with care, it can be used to haul pipes and wires through ducting, to hoist scaffold poles, or to form a slide and grip attachment to a pole or other rope.

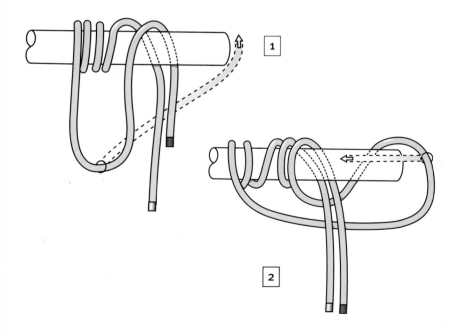

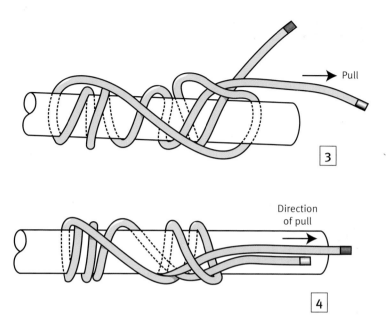

The method of tying shown here requires the end of the cylindrical object to be available, but having learned to tie it this way, carefully remove the two ends from the loop and you will see that by forming a crossing loop in the tying process the ends can be put through this to form the knot over a bar or rope where the end is not available.

Take the working end and form four or more turns away from the direction of pull, then, leaving a long loop, bring it back over the pole and lay it parallel to the standing part as in diagram 1. Now take the loop behind the standing part and the working end and slip it over the end of the pole. The knot should now look like diagram 3. Pull all the turns up close and tighten the knot before applying the pull in the direction shown in diagram 4.

Anchor Bend

The Anchor Bend, or Fisherman's Bend as it is sometimes known, is a stable and very reliable knot. It can be used to attach rope, cord, or even monofilament lines to a ring or bar as it pulls up snug; even after heavy loading, with a little persuasion, it can be untied. Typical uses include tying a rope to a small anchor, a berthing line to a ring, a swing rope to a branch, or a lead rope to a ring.

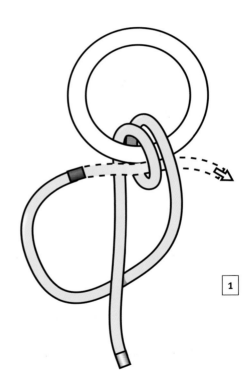

1

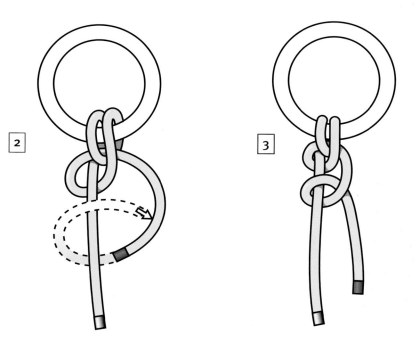

Take the working end and make a Round Turn loosely around the ring or bar. Pass the working end over the standing part then through the turns, before tying off with a Half Hitch around the standing part. To make the knot more secure a second Half Hitch can be added and if the knot is to remain in place for some while it would be prudent to seize the end to the standing part with a Flat Seizing (page 138). To untie after the knot has been under load, take off the Seizing and Half Hitch(es), then move the collar that is around the standing part away from the ring.

Prusik Knot

The Prusik Knot is used to attach a sling made from rope or tape to a climbing line, and works on a "Move and Grip" principle—the grip being from both the friction of the turns and the load forming a slight bend in the climbing rope. From there, the uses of this knot are almost limitless and can vary from a tie-in and climbing aid to a sling used as a becket from which tools, bags or coils of rope can be slung, moved, and held in a convenient place on either vertical or horizontal lines. If the sling is made using a knot make sure that this knot is away from the Prusik and not where the sling will be loaded.

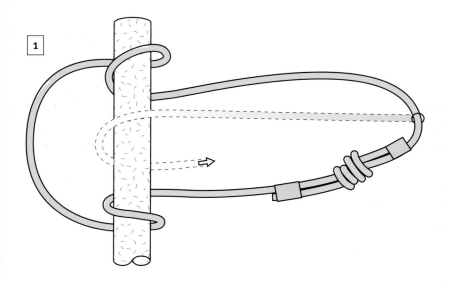

1

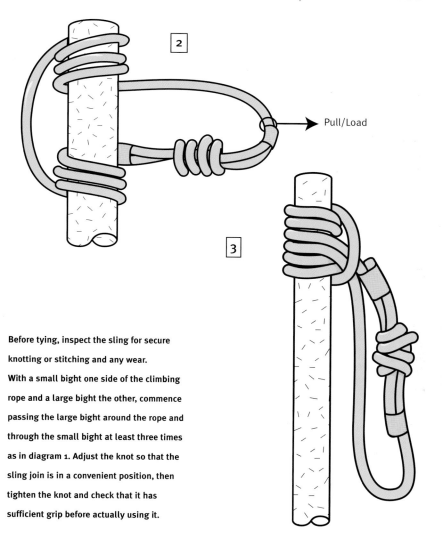

Before tying, inspect the sling for secure
knotting or stitching and any wear.
With a small bight one side of the climbing
rope and a large bight the other, commence
passing the large bight around the rope and
through the small bight at least three times
as in diagram 1. Adjust the knot so that the
sling join is in a convenient position, then
tighten the knot and check that it has
sufficient grip before actually using it.

Taut-Line Hitch

This is a Rolling Hitch (pages 162-163), tied around its own standing part or another rope. The difference being that the two ends exit from the knot in the same direction. Thought to have originated in the agriculture industry, it has many uses for securing lines to ropes or as shown here it can be used as a light guy line for tents, awnings, canopies, etc.

Make a crossing loop, then take two turns inside the loop before crossing to the standing part and applying a Half Hitch in the direction shown.

1

Tree Surgeon's Knot

Akin to the Taut-line Hitch, the Tree Surgeon's Knot is the same but with one extra turn, which allows a load to be applied to either of the two ends. Primarily a pull and grip knot, it can be used to support and lower a branch or bough of a tree. Like most of the Rolling Hitches, this one also needs to be used with caution, as it can "roll round" causing the end to pull through.

Make a round turn around the branch to the right of the standing part. Bring the working end round in front of the standing part and make another round turn to the left of the standing part, but in the opposite direction.

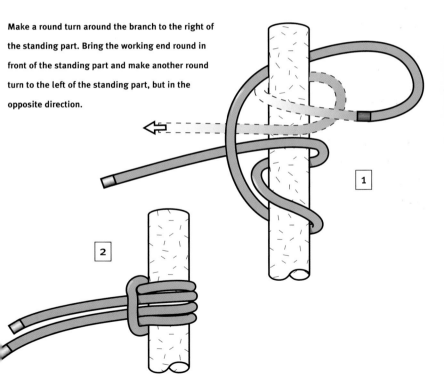

Blake's Hitch

Blake's Hitch is an alternative to the Taut-Line Hitch and because it does not bind as heavily as the Taut-Line Hitch, it appears to cause less friction damage to the ropes. It still needs to be used with caution, and a stopper knot in the working end is essential to stop it from pulling out if the knot rolls.

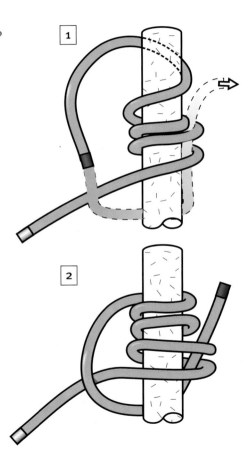

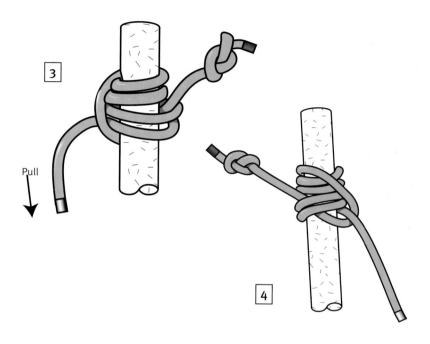

Hold the climbing rope in one hand with your thumb laid along the rope. Make two turns (with the tying-in rope) around the rope and your thumb, then two more turns above the thumb. Bring the working end back over the standing part and behind the climbing rope, take your thumb from the first two turns and insert the working end up through them, as shown in diagram 1. Tie a Figure of Eight Knot near the end of the working end, pulling it up to form a secure stopper knot. If you look at diagram 4 showing the knot tied, you will see that if the standing part is pulled around the rear of the climbing line, to the left, it will pull the end through if it does not have this stopper knot in it.

Towing Hitch

If you have to tow a vehicle that does not have a suitable towing point at the front, it is probable that you will have to crawl under it, find a suitable anchor point, and then try to tie the tow line in a very confined space. This Towing Hitch is designed to alleviate that problem by bringing the knot out to the front of the vehicle where it is not only easier to tie, but can be seen and checked regularly.

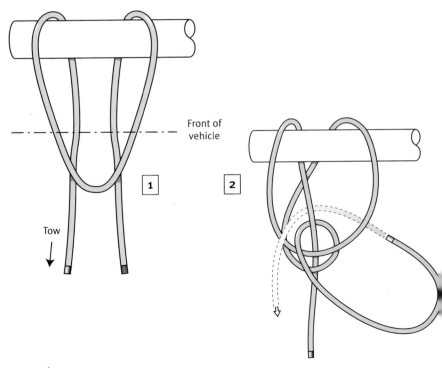

Front of vehicle

Tow

1

2

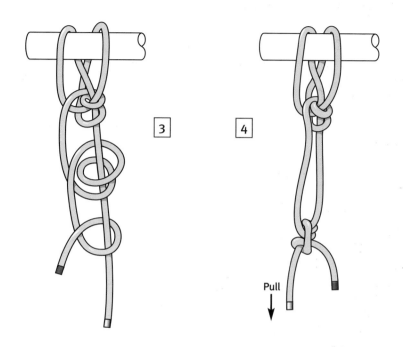

3   **4**

Pull

Make a very long bight in the end of the towing rope by doubling it. Take the bight under the vehicle and pass it around a suitable towing point then back out to the front as in diagram 1. Pass the working end over the standing part and through the bight, twice, before pulling up on both the working end and the standing part. Now secure the working end with a Midshipman's Hitch around the standing part and tighten up—this will now take the weight of the line from the two turns and stop them from slipping. Commence the tow slowly to tighten the whole arrangement, check that it is holding, then proceed with the tow.

High Post Hitch

As its name implies, the High Post Hitch is a means of securing a line to a post or bollard that may be out of reach when you want to release the line. This can be particularly useful for berthing lines where the tidal range is more than a few feet. It can also be used for lowering (inanimate) objects like bags or branches from a height so that you can recover the line and use it again without having to have somebody to help on the ground.

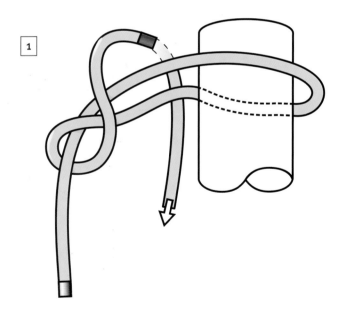

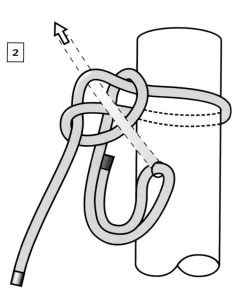

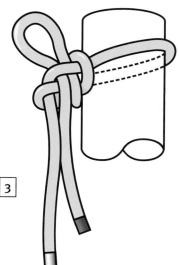

Pass a long bight, or long end, over or around the bollard or other object. Make a crossing turn around the standing part then back behind both legs of the bight as in diagram 1. Form a bight in the working end and tuck that between the crossover and the standing part as in diagram 2. Pull on the standing part to tighten the knot—pull on the working end to release it.

Knots at the End of a Rope

Introduction

There are two main categories of knots we use at the end of a piece of rope. Firstly the knots that prevent the rope's end from slipping out of an aperture or through a block or thimble—these are called "stopper knots." Then there are the knots that stop the end of a rope from fraying—these are "whipping."

The "stopper knots" range from a simple Overhand Knot to the decorative knob knots that we often see at the end of a banister or barrier rope. There is also the ever-popular Monkey's Fist, which started life as a weight for a heaving line, but because of its attractive symmetrical design, has become a much used knot for making key fobs, door stops, and even earrings and cuff links.

Another popular knot is the Matthew Walker Knot, which develops into an interesting spiral to gather together the ends of a plait or sinnet and either finishes it off or acts as a break point from which leads can emerge to change to another plait or sinnet.

Finally, we examine the "whipping" of the end of a rope, which is necessary either as a temporary measure while working with the rope or strands, or as a permanent ending to stop the rope from unraveling.

List of Knots and Uses

GENERAL PURPOSE

OVERHAND KNOT—Small stopper knot in sewing threads, etc. **Page 184**

FOOTROPE KNOT—Decorative stopper knot at the end of a rope. **Page 190**

MANROPE KNOT—Decorative large stopper knot at the end of large ropes. **Page 192**

DIAMOND KNOT—Decorative under/over weave of three or more strands. **Page 196**

MATTHEW WALKER KNOT—Stopper knot in or near the end of a rope. Also decorative when made up from four or more strands or cords. **Page 198**

TEMPORARY WHIPPING—Method of holding the strands of a rope together while splicing or cutting, etc. **Page 200**

WEST COUNTRY WHIPPING—Quick half knot whipping around a rope end. **Page 201**

COMMON WHIPPING—Quick easy wrap to prevent the end of a rope fraying. **Page 202**

SAILMAKER'S WHIPPING—A permanent whipping in three strand rope. **Page 204**

PALM AND NEEDLE WHIPPING—A permanent whipping for stranded and braided ropes. **Page 206**

FRENCH WHIPPING—Decorative Half Hitch whipping. **Page 208**

CAMPING & CLIMBING

STEVEDORE'S KNOT—Large stopper knot that can be used as a knob at the end of a tree swing rope. **Page 186**

OYSTERMAN'S KNOT—Stopper knot for rope. **Page 187**

BOATING

FIGURE OF EIGHT—Stopper knot to prevent the ends of lines from going through blocks. **Page 184**

MONKEY'S FIST—Knot to weight the end of a Heaving Line. **Page 188**

HEAVING LINE KNOT—Form a quickly made weighted end on a throwing line. **Page 194**

Overhand and Figure of Eight Stopper Knots

Here is a reminder of the most elementary of the small end stopper knots that were in the Foundation Knots section. The Overhand Knot (diagram 1) and the Slipped Overhand Knot (diagram 2) are most suited to cottons and light cords. The Double Overhand Knot (diagram 3) and the Multiple Overhand Knot (diagram 4) are more suitable in monofilament line, cord, light line, and small diameter ropes. The Figure of Eight Knot (diagram 5), as a stopper knot, is suitable for ropes and lines of most types and commonly used at the end of sheets and halyards.

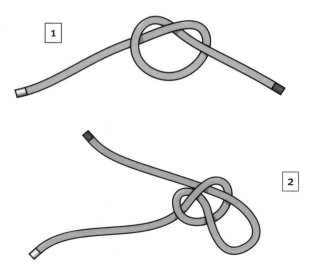

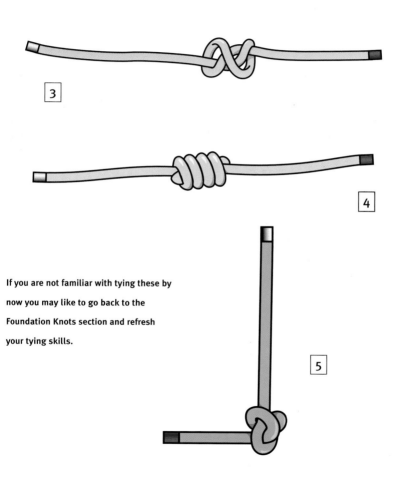

3

4

If you are not familiar with tying these by
now you may like to go back to the
Foundation Knots section and refresh
your tying skills.

5

Stevedore's Knot *Also known as Figure Nine*

The Stevedore's Knot or Figure Nine, as it is sometimes called, creates a slightly larger stopper knot in the end of a rope than a Figure of Eight Knot.

It is useful in small lines, but almost impossible to pull up in the heavier ropes.

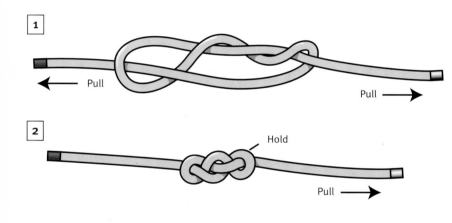

Start by doubling the working end back on the standing part. Take two turns around the standing part, then tuck the working end through the loop in the end, as shown in diagram 1. To begin, pull the knot up with both ends, then finish off by holding the base of the knot where the standing part enters it, then pull on the standing part to snug the knot up.

Oysterman's Knot

Named by Clifford Ashley, because he first saw it on an oyster boat, the Oysterman's Knot makes a slightly larger stopper again. It is ideal for putting a quick stopper knot on the end of a rope swing, or through a tent guy-line tensioning device.

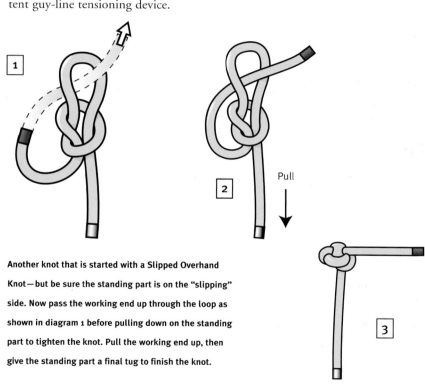

Another knot that is started with a Slipped Overhand Knot—but be sure the standing part is on the "slipping" side. Now pass the working end up through the loop as shown in diagram 1 before pulling down on the standing part to tighten the knot. Pull the working end up, then give the standing part a final tug to finish the knot.

Monkey's Fist Knot

The handsome Monkey's Fist Knot provides a weighted end to a heaving or throwing line. This knot should NEVER be formed around a hard heavy object if it is being used on the end of a heaving line. However, because of its symmetry it has become very popular as a decorative knot for making key fobs, door stops, earrings, cuff links, etc., where hard cores are sometimes used. Shown here is a Monkey's Fist tied in the traditional way with three sets of three turns. If tied around a spherical object, for decorative purposes, the three sets of turns may need more leads to cover it completely.

Start by roughly measuring the amount of line you will need to tie the Monkey's Fist—either wrap the line around your hand nine times (3 x 3) and then add a little (there will be no waste), or, if you are covering a sphere, wind the cord onto it, to estimate how much it will take to cover. Commence by making three turns loosely around the hand clockwise as in diagram 1. Then, holding the first three turns with your thumb and forefinger, wrap three more turns in a clockwise direction at 90 degrees to the first three, as in diagram 2.

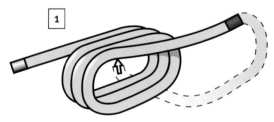

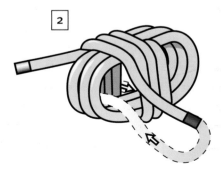

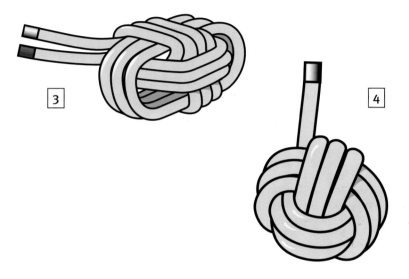

The next three turns are made inside the first three and outside the second three from the bottom to the top. Note the path of the working end indicated by the arrowed line when stage 2 is completed. The working end should then emerge alongside the standing part. At this stage you can either put a Figure of Eight Knot in the working end and tuck it into the middle of the knot, or leave it free to be spliced or seized to the standing part when the knot has been pulled up. To pull the knot up, start from the working end, using small adjustments (it may take two or three complete rounds to achieve the best result), push the line towards the knot, then pull the resulting loop a little, push the other side of the loop into the knot and pull the resulting loop and so on in sequence until you reach the standing part. Repeat (you may need the help of a spike towards the end) until a nice firm knot is achieved.

Footrope Knot

The Footrope Knot is in fact a Double Diamond Knot that is used on the footrope of a yardarm to prevent the feet slipping sideways, but with so few square-rigged ships around now it is perhaps more commonly used as a decorative knot in or at the end of a rope. Do not be deterred by the complicated look of this knot; it really is quite easy to tie, as you will discover.

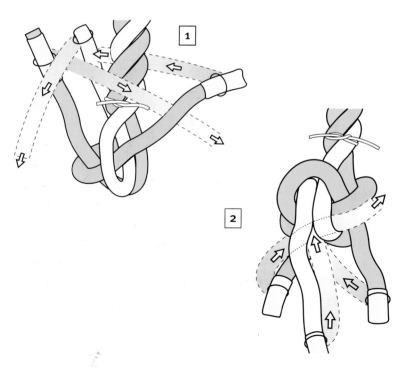

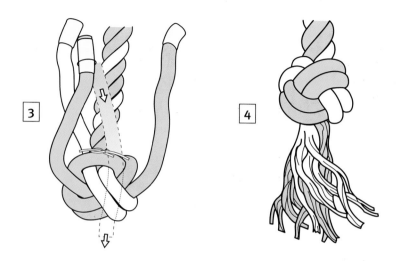

Practice using a piece of 3 strand rope to start with. Put a temporary whipping (page 200) on the rope about 15 times the diameter from the end. Un-lay the strands and tape or whip the ends. Form a loose Wall Knot (page 41) so that the ends of each strand lay up alongside the rope, as shown in diagram 1. Now Crown Knot the strands on top of the Wall Knot, as shown in diagram 2. Hold the uppermost part of the rope and you will see that the ends of the strands now lay with their own part. Tuck each strand alongside its own lead until it emerges up by the rope before tucking it down through the middle of the knot, as shown in diagram 3. The three strands now emerge from the center of the bottom of the knot. Tighten the knot by working from the rope, gradually tightening the knot up a little at a time. When the knot is firm, the three ends can be re-laid to form the rope again, whipped, or splayed out and combed into a tassel as shown here.

Manrope Knot

The Manrope Knot is yet another popular knot that we have inherited from the days of sail. It is similar to the Footrope Knot, but with the ends emerging from the rope side of the knot, making it an ideal "end of rope" knot. Today you are more likely to see it at the end of a stair rope, or a rope railing around the garden decking. The rhyme for remembering how to tie this knot goes: "First a Wall, and then a Crown, double it up by following round."

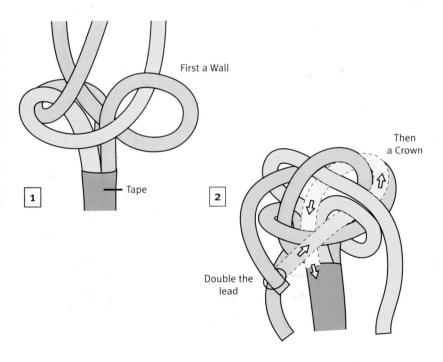

First a Wall

Then a Crown

1   — Tape

2

Double the lead

3

And tuck it
down

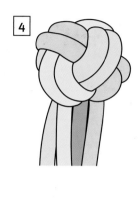

4

Tie a temporary whipping at about 15 times the diameter of
the rope from the working end, then un-lay the strands and
tape or whip the ends. Form a Wall Knot with the three
strands, as shown in diagram 1. Crown over the top of the
Wall Knot, as shown in diagram 2. Then double the lead, as
shown by the arrowed line. When all three are doubled, tuck
the end, as shown in diagram 3, into the middle of the knot
and out alongside the rope beside itself. Next, gradually
tighten the knot, little by little, until it forms a uniform
shape, then either splice the three strands back into the
standing part, or put on a Common Whipping as shown here.

5

Heaving Line Knot

Next to the Monkey's Fist, the Heaving Line Knot is the most appropriate weight for the end of a heaving or throwing line. It is quick and easy to tie, and even when wet and pulled up tight it can be untied. As a decorative knot, it will provide a knob at the end of a light pull or robe cord, but the Multiple Overhand Knot is better if it is to be permanent.

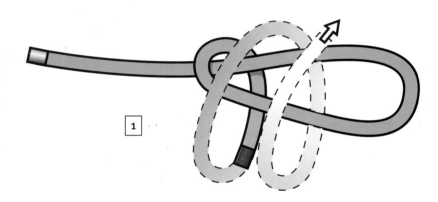

Form a large bight at the end of the line. Wrap the working end around the bight, as shown in diagram 1, using as many turns as the working end will go, before tucking it through the loop of the bight. Now, pull gently on the side of the loop to pull the first turn up snug against the others.

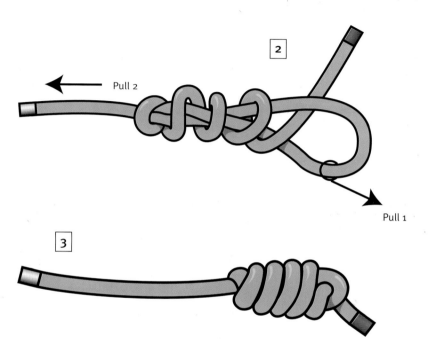

Make sure the wraps are fairly tight, then, holding the knot in one hand, pull the standing part until the working end is securely entrapped. The knot is now ready for use. To untie, hold the knot in one hand and pull the working end away from the knot until the loop enlarges; withdraw the working end and the wraps will come untied.

Diamond Knot

The Diamond Knot is another attractive crossing knot that can be used either in or at the end of stranded rope. Now primarily used as a decorative knot for lanyards and bell ropes, it can also be tied with more than three leads. When tied in a rope it resembles a Turk's Head Knot with an under-over-under sequence of crossings.

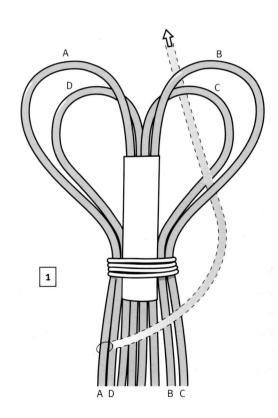

1

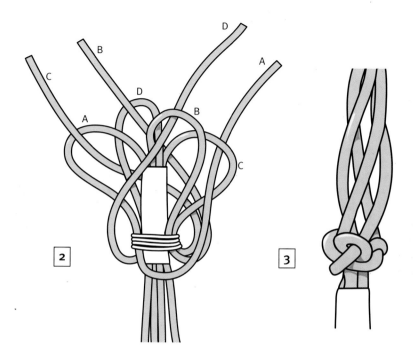

This example shows how to tie a Diamond Knot using four strands as if it were tied with the cords at the end of something like a sinnet. Double back the four leads and hold them to the core structure with a rubber band or constrictor knot. Take lead A and pass it over lead B and up under lead C, take B over C and up under D and so on until you arrive at stage 2. Now pull all four leads together, while holding the standing part of the structure. You may need to tease the knot into shape while you are doing so. From here you can either continue with another sinnet or tease the ends into a tassel.

Matthew Walker Knot

This is another end knot that can be utilized in decorative work, much the same as the Diamond Knot, except that the Matthew Walker Knot has an entirely different look about it. It too can be tied in three or more leads, so here, like the Diamond Knot, it is shown tied with four leads. This is a difficult knot to pull up until you get used to it, so if it does not look like the diagram the first time you attempt it (you will not be the first), try again—it really is worth it in the end.

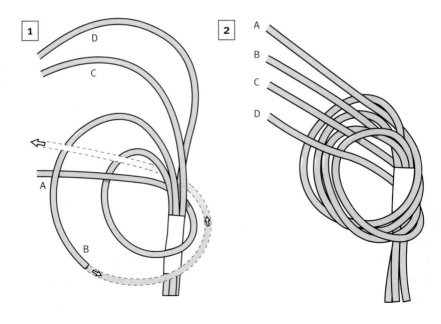

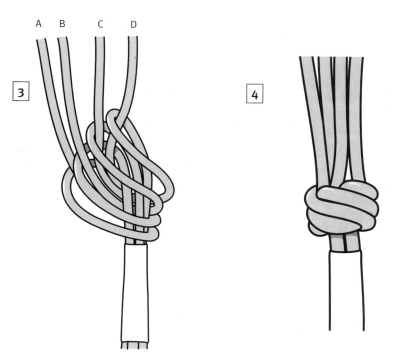

Tape or put a temporary whipping on the rope or sinnet where you want the knot to rest. Take the left hand lead and pass the working end round to the left, around the core, and up through itself, as shown in diagram 1. Repeat this process with all the leads and you should end up with a loose knot like that shown in diagram 2. Hold the core and gently pull on the ends of the leads all together, until you get to stage 3. Starting with the lead marked A, very gradually pull each lead a fraction in turn, at the same time teasing the turns around the knot into place. Giving the core a little twist sometimes helps to make pulling the knot up a little easier.

Temporary Whipping

The two most common temporary whippings are the Constrictor Knot and Double Constrictor Knot and tape. Ordinary masking tape is sufficient for most jobs, but electrical or climber's tape is better.

Temporary whipping is employed to prevent a rope from un-laying when splicing, or when you are working with individual strands or cutting rope. Shown here is the Double Constrictor Knot and two pieces of tape between which the rope will be cut.

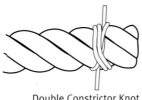

Double Constrictor Knot

West Country Whipping

West Country Whipping is another quick and easy whipping that can be applied to the end of any rope that is not too slippery. Best tied with waxed whipping twine, it should cover about one to one and a half times the diameter of the rope.

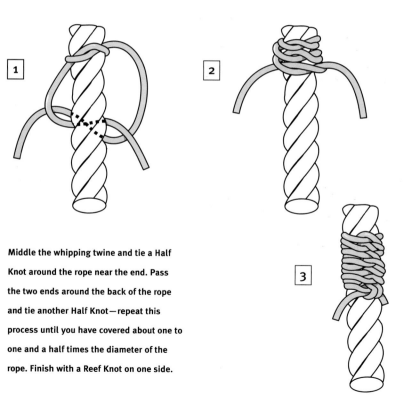

Middle the whipping twine and tie a Half Knot around the rope near the end. Pass the two ends around the back of the rope and tie another Half Knot—repeat this process until you have covered about one to one and a half times the diameter of the rope. Finish with a Reef Knot on one side.

Common Whipping

The Common Whipping shown here is quick and easy to apply and can be used as a permanent finish to the end of most ropes. However, it is not recommended for use on Nylon or Polypropylene ropes as it can slide off.

Pre-waxed whipping twine is the best, but a length of jute garden twine or similar line, drawn across some beeswax or candlewax, will also do the job.

1

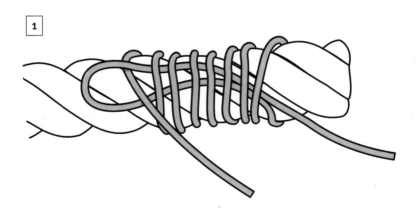

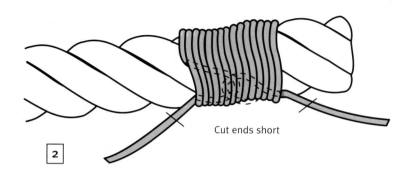

Cut ends short

2

Diagram 1 has been tied "open" so that you can follow the instructions. Lay a bight along the rope as shown in diagram 1, then make a series of turns around the rope, as tight and close as possible, to cover about one to one and a half times the diameter of the rope. Pass the working end through the loop in the bight. Pull both ends of the whipping twine to keep them tight then draw the loop into the center of the whipping, as shown by the dotted lines in diagram 2, before cutting off the ends.

3

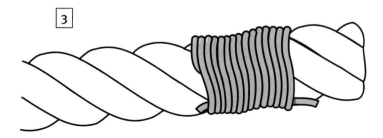

Sailmaker's Whipping

The favorite of sailors for finishing the end of a stranded rope is the Sailmaker's Whipping. It not only looks nice, it also holds very well, especially if it is put on tight with waxed twine. Like other whipping, it should be applied near the end of the rope and be about one to one and a half times the diameter of the rope.

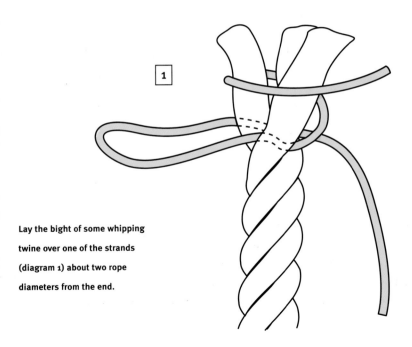

1

Lay the bight of some whipping twine over one of the strands (diagram 1) about two rope diameters from the end.

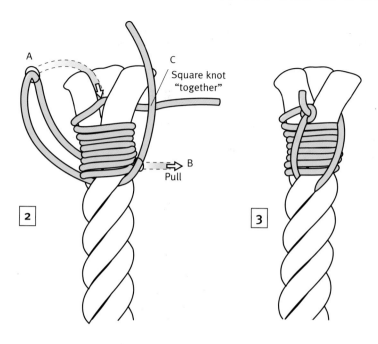

A

C
Square knot
"together"

B
Pull

2

3

Take the long end and make tight close turns around the rope, working towards the end, for about one to one and a half times the diameter of the rope—end on the strand that the loop is on, then pass the twine between this strand and the one to the right of it, as shown in diagram 2. To finish the whipping, take the loop (A) and place it over the strand that it straddles—pull it down tight with its end (B) then tie the two ends (C) together with a Reef Knot in the center of the strands. Trim the end of the rope.

Palm and Needle Whipping

Palm and Needle Whipping is the only permanent whipping suitable for core and braid ropes. It can also be used on stranded rope but the method shown here is specifically for braids. You will need waxed twine and a needle with a sufficiently large eye, and ideally a sailmaker's palm, although this may not be required on many of the braid on braid ropes. One important thing to remember is to first "balance" the rope—put your hand around the rope about six feet from the end and draw it towards the end; this ensures that both the core and cover are not bunched up anywhere and that they both take an even weight of any load.

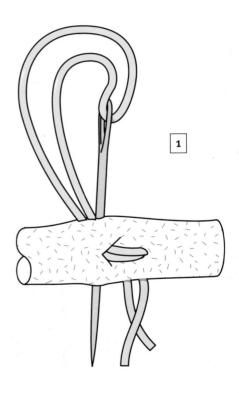

1

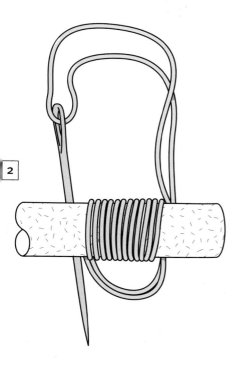

Load a suitable needle with whipping twine, and double sew the cover and core together—back to front then side to side at 90 degrees, as shown in diagram 1. Lay the ends along the rope, then make a series of tight turns (over the ends) around the rope for about one and a half times the diameter of the rope. At the end, push the needle through the center of the rope so that it emerges close to the last turn on the other side. Enter the rope again at the other end of the whipping and go back through the center of the rope—repeat this turn around the whipping from bottom to top as shown in diagram 2, then tie off using two Half Hitches over these. Pass the needle through the rope once more, pull and cut the ends so that they shrink back into the rope.

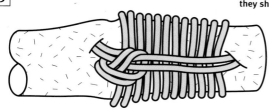

French Whipping

French Whipping is a series of Half Hitches around a rope end, which provides a reliable whipping and with it a decorative spiral around the rope. Suitable for stranded, braided, or multiplait rope. As with most whipping, it should be close to the end and be about one to one and a half times the diameter of the rope.

1

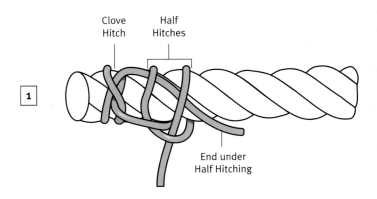

Clove Hitch

Half Hitches

End under Half Hitching

2

Pull to draw
overhand knot up tight ⟶

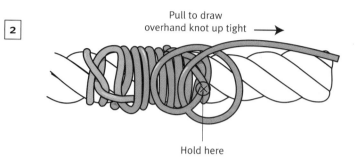

Hold here

Start with a Clove Hitch around the rope near
the end, as shown in diagram 1. Tuck the short
end along the rope then Half Hitch over the rope
(and the end) as tight and close as possible
until you have covered sufficient rope. Finish off
with a Clove Hitch pulled up tight, then make an
Overhand Knot, as shown in diagram 2, holding
the point where the twine exits the Clove Hitch
with your finger and pulling on the end—this
ensures the knot is up close to the Clove Hitch
and will stop it from coming untied. Lose the
end in the lay of the rope and cut it off.

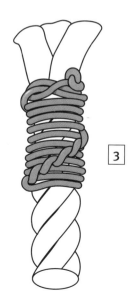

3

Splicing

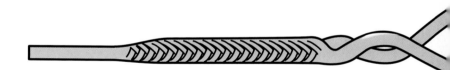

Introduction

Splicing is a form of knotting used at the end of a rope or for joining ropes, where knots are not practical, safe, or secure enough for the job. It is more professional to splice a rope that would otherwise require a knot to be tied in it every time it is used. Each different splice has its purpose, for example: a stopper knot would not go through a pulley block, so we use a Back Splice; a Bowline in a berthing hawser would weaken it considerably, so we use an Eye Splice; a Sheet Bend in the end of a halyard would prevent it from being hauled close up to a block, so we use an Eye Splice or a Ring Splice.

In this book, I have included only splices that can be learned from a book and can, with some ingenuity, be formed without specialist tools or equipment. The section starts with the time-honored conventional 3 strand rope splices. These were first devised for natural fiber ropes, and although most are suited to the now more common, man-made fibers, certain precautions are needed to ensure that the splices are as effective in one as the other. An Eye Splice in natural fiber rope may only need three tucks, whereas in Nylon it will need five tucks and even then may need additional whipping or dogging to ensure that it is safe, secure, and stable. Another fairly recent and popular rope in the maritime world is the multiplait rope, which is normally either eight or twelve strands made up in pairs, half of which are right hand laid, the other half left hand laid. The method of splicing this rope to make an eye or to join ends is shown on pages 224–227. Then there are the braided ropes; either with no core, with a core of another braid, or with cores of many other differing designs and materials—each requiring their own brand of splice that must be carefully executed using specialist tools. The braided rope splices shown in this section are included only to show how they are done. If you are going to use these in practical situations you should consult the rope manufacturer's data for recommended splices.

List of Knots and Uses

Three Strand Back Splice

The Back Splice is a quick method of terminating the end of a rope to stop it from fraying—especially where a stopper knot would prevent the rope from roving through a block or eye.

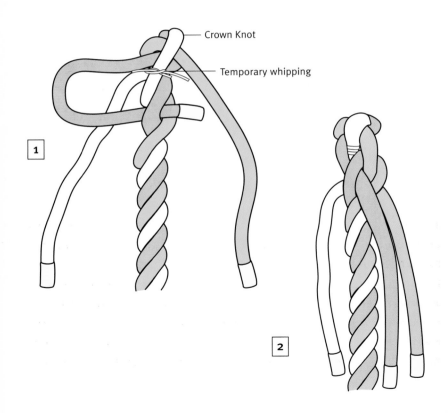

Crown Knot

Temporary whipping

1

2

3

4

Strength is not an issue with the Back Splice, therefore the number of tucks is normally three or four in any stranded rope. Commence by putting a temporary whipping or tape at the point where the Back Splice is to start—un-lay the strands up to this point. Crown the ends over the temporary whipping as in diagram 1. Now commence an "over one strand, under one strand" sequence with each of the three strands in turn. When the first tuck has been made with all three strands, as shown in diagram 2, remove the temporary whipping and pull the strands up tight to the Crown Knot. Complete the required number of tucks, pulling each set up tight as you go. Taper or whip the ends. One method of finishing a Three Strand Splice is shown here—miss one strand, tuck the next one once, and the third one twice.

Three Strand Eye Splice

An Eye Splice forms a fixed loop in the end of a rope. This splice also retains most of the strength of the rope, whereas a knot would weaken the rope considerably.

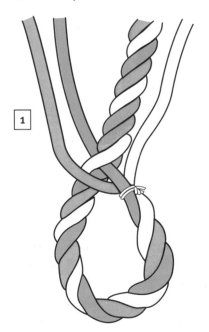

Measure enough rope from the end of the rope to make the required number of tucks, and a little spare for handling; apply a temporary whipping at this point. Bend the rope round to form the required eye—if this is to be around a thimble, lay the thimble on the rope and bend the rope round it as tight as you can, holding the thimble in place with at least three temporary whippings before you commence the splice. Un-lay the strands up to the temporary whipping and tape or whip the ends. Now lay the three strands across the rope as in diagram 1 and tuck the center one under one of the standing part strands. Next, take the strand on the left and go over the strand with the first tuck under it and under the next one. Turn the work over and you will see one standing part strand without a

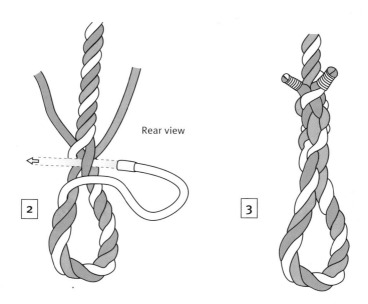

Rear view

2

3

working strand under it (see diagram 2) and tuck the remaining strand under this one as shown. Pull all three strands up neatly and snugly (under the thimble if one is being used). Check that the three working ends each emerge from between two standing part strands. Continue the "over one/under one" sequence with each strand in turn until the required number of tucks is complete. In large hawsers, especially those that will be subjected to jerking, like those used for berthing ships, it is wise to "dog" the ends. This is done by dividing each strand end into two parts and whipping two halves of adjacent strands on top of the standing part strand between them. Other splices can of course be tapered or whipped to suit the situation.

Three Strand Short Splice

A Short Splice is used to join two identical ropes' ends.
This is a strong splice but because it increases the
diameter considerably, the use of the rope will be limited.

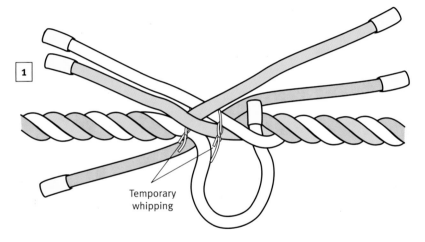

1

Temporary
whipping

Measure back from the two ends a sufficient distance for the required number of tucks and apply a
temporary whipping or tape around both ropes. Un-lay and tape the ends of the three strands in each
rope up to the point of the temporary whipping. Lay the two ropes together end to end, up to the
temporary whipping, interlacing the strands of one end between the strands of the other, as shown in
diagram 1. Now tuck the three ends of one rope into the standing strands of the other rope beyond the
temporary whipping—using the "over one, under one" sequence. Remove the tape/whipping, then pull
these strands up tight before tucking the three strands of the other rope into the other standing part

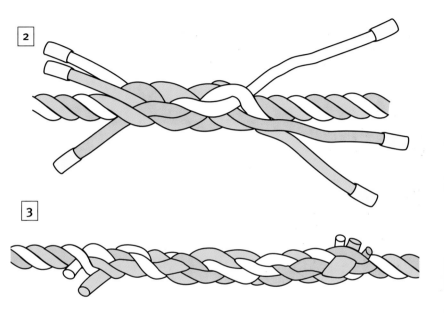

strands, as shown in diagram 2. Remove the tape/whipping from this side, then pull these up tight so that the two ropes lock together and equal strain is carried on all the strands. Complete the required number of tucks each side of the join and finish off with a taper—either by reducing the number of yarns in each strand or using the "leave one strand, tuck the next strand once, and the third strand twice" sequence. If the rope is likely to be pulled over an obstruction or through a fairlead, a whipping could be used over the ends of the splice to stop them from snagging.

Three Strand Long Splice

The Long Splice joins the ends of identical ropes without significant increase in thickness. Although not as strong as the Short Splice, the Long Splice is used where the rope needs to be led over a pulley wheel or through a block or eye.

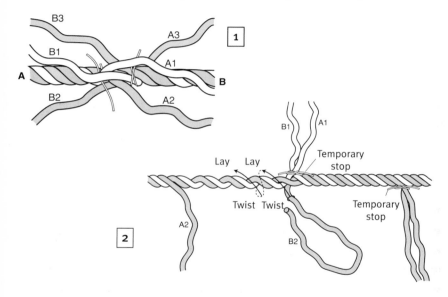

The illustrations for this description are limited by the page size and are therefore only representative of the principles used—the distance apart of the three join splices will be much greater than that shown. Count at least ten turns of one strand back from the end of each rope and apply a temporary whipping around each rope at this point. Un-lay the strands, up to the whipping. Lay the strands of rope A between the strands of rope B as shown in diagram 1.

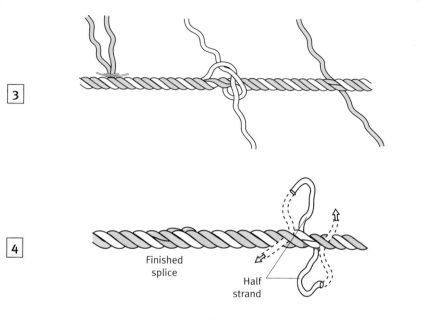

3

4

Finished
splice

Half
strand

Tie strands A1 and B1 together with a temporary whipping—these will be the center join splice
strands. Un-lay strand A2 and replace it with strand B2—twisting the strand and laying it in snug. At
about nine turns put a temporary whipping on both strands to hold them together. Repeat this to the
right with strands A3 and B3. At this point, and before commencing the splices, make sure that the
strands at the center point are balanced and that the lay of the rope is as it was before you started—
this ensures equal loading on each strand. Tie a Half Knot in strands A1 and B1, as shown in diagram 3,
so that the knot lies snug in the lay of the rope (as shown for A3–B3). Check again that A2–B2 and
A3–B3 are laid in snug—adjust as necessary. Now Half Knot the other two sets of strands. Stretch the
whole splice for a final check, and then complete each join splice by halving each strand end and
tucking the ends over/under/over as shown in diagram 4.

Three Strand Grommet

A Grommet is a rope ring that can be used for a variety of purposes from games to working strops. Particular uses for the Grommet include Quoits and Pucks for deck games, foundation eyelets for sewn (worked) eyes in canvas, rope handles, and rope strops.

Take a length of three strand rope three and a half to four times the length of the circumference of the grommet you wish to make. Each strand will make one Grommet. Carefully un-lay each strand from the rope, ensuring that you keep the spiral shape of the lay. Tie a Half Knot in the strand, as shown in diagram 1, ensuring that the knot lays snug in the lay and that the diameter of the loop is the correct size for the Grommet. You should now have two ends that are roughly the same length. Take one end and lay it back into the strand with a gentle twist as you go—it should now look like diagram 2.

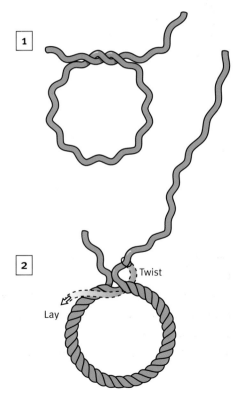

1

2

Twist

Lay

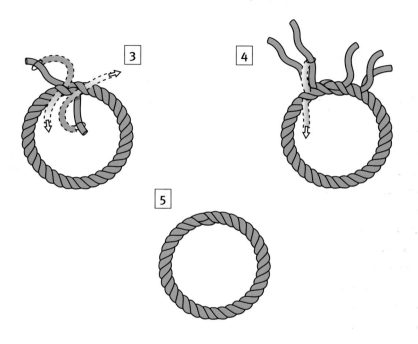

Now take the other end, and with a firmer twisting action lay it in next to the previous end to reform

the rope back to look like its original lay. The two ends will now be tied using a Half Knot that lies in

the lay of the rope as depicted in diagram 3. It helps if you can stretch the Grommet over a cone before

pulling this knot up really tight. If it does not lie snug, reduce the diameter of the two strand ends

until it does. Un-lay the strand ends, then remove more fibers, before tucking them

over/under/over/under like a normal splice, as shown in diagram 4.

Multi-Plait Eye Splice

Eight strand multiplait rope is made up of eight strands, in four pairs, plaited in a four strand square plait. Two pairs are right hand laid, the other two left hand laid—one of these pairs is quite often marked with a colored strand. As this form of rope is normally used for mooring or berthing ropes, an Eye Splice is preferred to a knot to retain the strength in the rope.

Keep in mind that the finished splice should look very much like the rope construction, only thicker. Measure enough length from the end to make at least five tucks; put on a temporary whipping or tape at this point. Un-lay the strands in their pairs and tape the ends. Measure and form the eye. Identify the two left and two right hand laid strands and lay them out as shown in diagram 1.

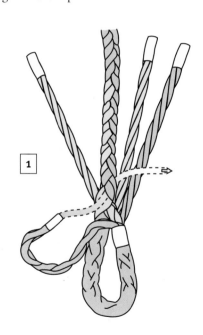

1

224

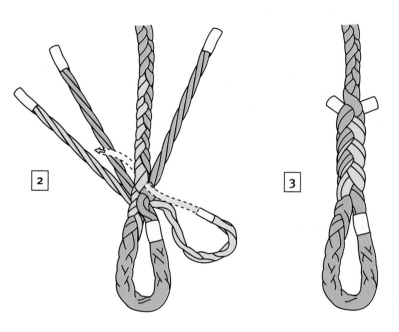

Tuck one of the right hand laid pair under a convenient right hand standing strand pair, in the direction shown in the diagram. Turn the eye over and tuck the other right hand pair under the remaining right hand standing part strands. Repeat with the two left hand laid pairs, always laying on top of the opposite lay and tucking under the same lay. When the five tucks are completed it is advisable to "dog" the ends—take the tape from the pairs and separate them. Marry one right and one left strand over the top of the standing strand between them and put on a secure whipping. Repeat for the other strands.

Multi-Plait Short Splice

The Eight Plait Short Splice is used to join two identical
ropes together.

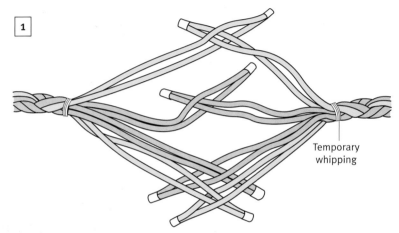

Temporary
whipping

Measure from the end of each rope enough length to make at least five tucks; put on a temporary

whipping or tape at this point. Un-lay the strands in their pairs and tape the ends. Lay the two ropes

end to end with the strand pairs laid out as in diagram 1. Interlace like for like strands as shown, then

pull all four ends to bring the two ropes together as in diagram 2. Put a temporary whipping over the

join, around all the strands. Tuck a right hand laid pair of strands under a left hand laid standing part

pair, then turn the work and repeat. Tuck a left hand laid pair under a right hand standing part pair in

the directions shown in diagram 3. Continue to lay over like and tuck under opposite, for five tucks.

Then either taper the ends as in the left of the final diagram, or "dog" the ends in the same way as for

the Eye Splice.

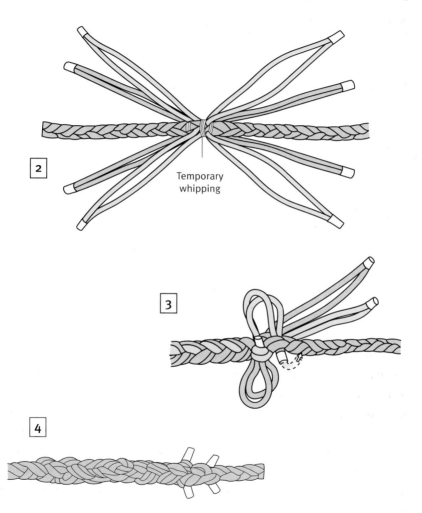

2

Temporary
whipping

3

4

Rope to Chain Splice

Because of multiplait rope's popularity for anchor lines, it is often spliced to an anchor chain. There are (at least) two schools of thought for completing this splice—one that leaves the splice exposed, so that the splice can be seen and inspected before use and allows the chain to act almost as flexibly as it would without a splice—the disadvantage being that it wears the rope quicker. The other is to serve over the splice to form a tight bond between the rope and chain—the disadvantages being that the spliced portion is stiff and will not carry round a small capstan or winch, that it cannot be inspected, and that the rope under the serving is difficult to dry out. Clear shrink-wrap tubing can be a fair compromise.

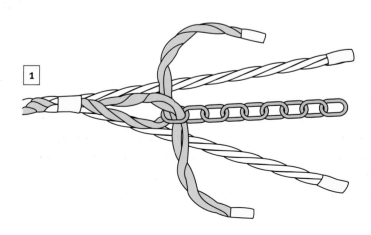

1

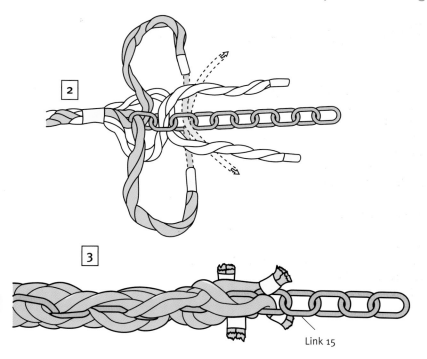

Link 15

Measure off the rope for the span of about fifteen links of chain, put a temporary whipping at this point and un-lay the pairs of strands, taping the ends as you go. Lay the strands out as in diagram 1—note that the marked pair are crossed inside the unmarked pair. Thread the ends of the marked pair through the first link in opposite directions as shown in diagram 2 and pull up to the whipping. Take the unmarked pair and thread them through the next link in the same manner. Continue for at least six tucks with each pair, then remove the tape from the ends and split the pairs. Marry a left hand and right hand strand and "dog" them together with a strong whipping, repeating for all four pairs.

Rope to Ring Splice

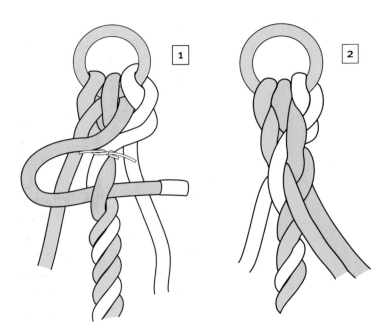

Measure enough to form at least three tucks from the end of the rope and apply a temporary

whipping. Tape the ends of each strand and un-lay them up to the whipping. Now, rather like the

Eye Splice, start with the middle strand and pass that through the ring and back alongside itself to

the right. Take the strand to the left of that and pass it in the same manner beside the first.

3

The remaining strand now goes through the ring and back alongside itself, then is tucked from front to back to the left of itself, as shown in diagram 1.

Commence the "over one, under one" sequence of the splice with the center strand. Lead it over the right strand on the standing part side of the temporary whipping and tuck under the next, as shown in diagram 2. Now tuck the left hand strand under the standing part of the right hand strand, then the right hand strand under the standing part strand that is vacant around the back of the splice. Complete the required number of tucks, pulling up tight each round as you go. Finish with a taper, whipping or just cut the ends up close.

Hollow Braid Adjustable Eye Splice

The Adjustable Eye Splice is quick and very easy to make in true hollow braided ropes—but be aware that some ropes that look hollow may not be flexible enough to take an end back down through the center.

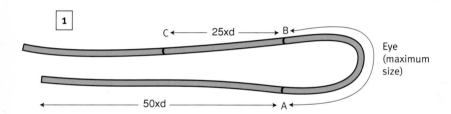

Multiply the diameter of the rope by 50; measure that distance from the end of the rope and mark it A (use a chinagraph pencil, highlighter, or marker pen). Make a second mark B at the maximum circumference of the eye required. Add a third mark C at 25 times the diameter from the eye along the standing part.

The next step is to pull the end through from mark B to mark C, as shown in diagram 2.

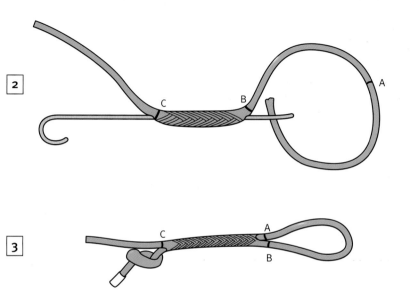

A Marlow splicing needle is shown in the diagram; however if you do not have one of these, use a piece of stiff wire bent into a loop, or a length of whipping twine passed through with a needle will also work. Bunch the rope from the standing part toward the eye to make passage of the end easier. Bring the end out at mark C, adjust the loop to the required size and tie off the end with an Overhand Knot as a stopper knot. Pull back on the eye and the splice is complete.

Hollow Braid Tucked Eye Splice

The Tucked Eye Splice is intended for use in true hollow braid ropes to form a permanent fixed eye. The method shown here is only one of several variations to achieve this.

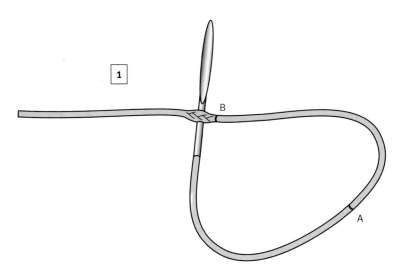

Multiply the diameter of the rope by 50 and put a mark "A" on the rope, as for the previous splice.

Measure the eye and make a second mark "B" as shown. Pass the end of the rope right through the

standing part at mark B, as shown in diagram 1. Again, this diagram shows the ideal tool for the job,

but because the rope is so flexible it is easily done with a fid, or even by taping the end to a ballpoint

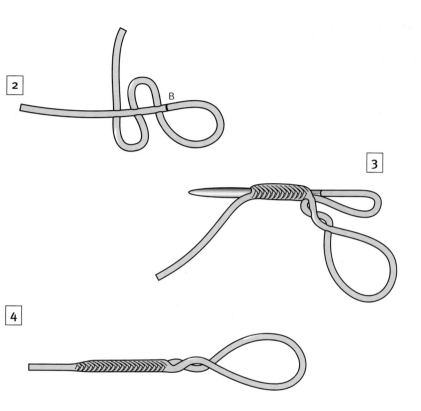

pen. Pass the end through the rope three times, as shown in diagram 2. Complete the splice by pulling the end so that the eye is the required size and the two first tucks are tight—then taper the end, bunch up the standing part toward the eye, and feed the end into the center of the rope at the point where the third tuck exited.

Double Braid Eye Splice

Also known as Braid on Braid

Double Braid, or Braid on Braid as it is sometimes known, takes a splice quite easily, but it does take practice. A few things to remember—don't think you will get it right first time; if you do you will probably be the first! Don't try to splice old, used rope; the core will have been contorted and misused so much that it will give you trouble right from the start. Don't learn to splice with rope under about ⁵⁄₁₆ inch (8 mm) diameter. Do consult the manufacturer's instructions for appropriate splicing information.

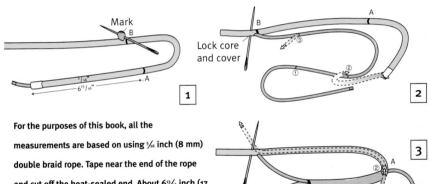

For the purposes of this book, all the measurements are based on using ⁵⁄₁₆ inch (8 mm) double braid rope. Tape near the end of the rope and cut off the heat-sealed end. About 6¹³⁄₁₆ inch (17 cm) from the end, mark the rope "A," as shown in diagram 1, then form an eye to the required size and mark the rope here, "B." At about 4½ feet (1.5 meters) from the end of the rope, tie a knot (Alpine Butterfly is a good one) in the standing part, as you will need to secure it to a strong point at a later stage—this also allows you to work the cover up and down the core and vice versa. Carefully open the weave at mark "B" by pushing aside complete sets of threads (picks)—make sure they are complete; just one fiber left on the wrong side will cause a lot of grief. Pick out the core with a needle or end of a fid, then pull it out from the cover completely. Smooth the cover over the core, working from the knot to mark "B" in order to

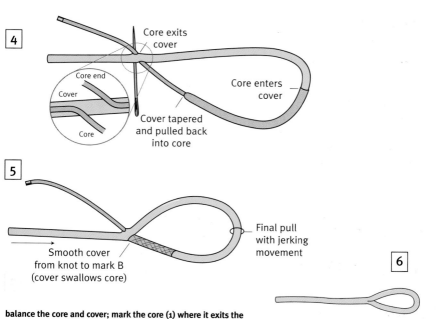

4 Core exits cover · Core end · Cover · Core · Cover tapered and pulled back into core · Core enters cover

5 Smooth cover from knot to mark B (cover swallows core) · Final pull with jerking movement

6

balance the core and cover; mark the core (1) where it exits the

cover at "B." Pull out as much core as you can from the standing part of the cover and lock the two with a

needle or small spike—this is not essential, but it does make the job easier. On the core, measure 6¹³⁄₁₆ inch

(17 cm) from (1) toward the standing part and mark it (2), measure a further 4¹³⁄₁₆ inch (12 cm) a make a mark

(3). Using a splicing fid or needle (or wire loop/twine) feed the cover into the core at (2) and out at (3) as

shown in diagrams 2 and 3. Feed the end of the core into the cover near mark "A" and exit just on the

standing part side of mark "B." Remove the locking needle. Taper the end of the cover and pull it back into

the core by smoothing the core over the cover towards the standing part and at the same time pulling the

end of the core at mark "B" to smooth out the whole arrangement so that it looks like diagram 4. Complete

the splice by milking the cover from the knot towards mark "B" so that it swallows the exposed core from

(3) to where it enters the cover at "A." The final stage is to attach the knot to a strong point, insert a fid or

handle in the eye and give it a good sharp pull. Cut off the excess core and shrink it back into the cover.

Double Braid End or Back Splice

An End or Back Splice in double braid rope is a neat and secure way of ensuring the end will not fray—it also avoids abrasion caused by the hard edges of a hot knife cut, especially if the end is likely to pass through a gripped hand.

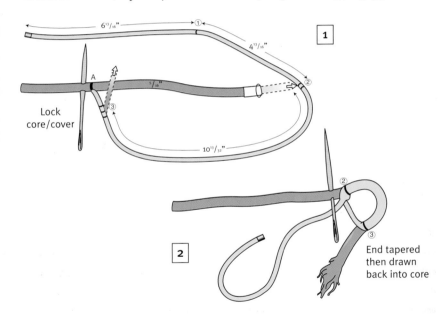

Lock core/cover

End tapered then drawn back into core

Tape the end of the rope and cut off the heat-sealed end. Tie a knot about 5 feet (1.5 meters) from the end. Measure 6₁₃/₁₆ inch (17 cm) from the end and mark the rope A. Remove the core at mark A, smooth cover from the knot to mark A and mark the core (1) at the point where it exits mark A. Pull out as much

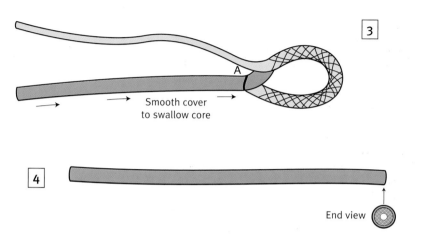

Smooth cover
to swallow core

End view

core as you can and lock the core and cover together on the standing side of mark A. Measure a

distance of $4_{13/16}$ inch (12 cm) along the exposed core from (1) and mark it (2), then a further $10_{13/32}$

inch (26 cm) and mark it (3), as shown in diagram 1. Feed the cover into the core at (2) and out at (3) —

the arrangement will now look like diagram 2. Taper the end of the cover, then work the core over it

until it is buried in the core. Smooth the cover from the knot towards mark A, making sure that the

exposed portion of the core does not bunch up. Repeat until the exposed core over the cover is buried

in the standing part of the cover. Cut off the excess core end and make one final smoothing of the cover

until the core parts are completely buried and the end is a neat ring of braided cover.

Braid and Core Splice

Be aware that this example of a Braid and Core Splice is but one of many used in braided rope with a core that is not a braid. Before splicing any rope of this kind you should obtain the manufacturer's data on how to splice it.

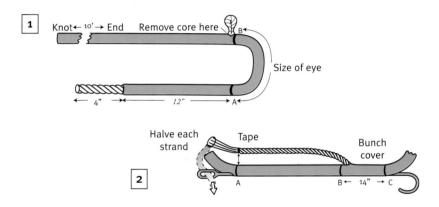

Tie a knot (Alpine Butterfly) about 10 feet (3 meters) from the end of the rope. Tape near the end and cut off the heat-sealed end. Pull the core from the end of the cover out about 4 inches (10 cm), hold the two together, then milk the cover back up towards the knot for about 3 feet (1 meter) or so. Measure 12 inches (30 cm) from the end of the cover and mark A, the form the eye and mark the other side at mark B. Remove the core at mark B, then smooth the cover from the knot to mark B to balance the core and cover. Tape the core opposite mark A, then un-lay the remainder of the core and taper it by halving each strand, applying one layer of thin smooth tape to hold the ends. Measure 14 inches (35 cm) from mark B toward the knot and mark this at mark C, as shown in diagram 2. Now bunch up the cover

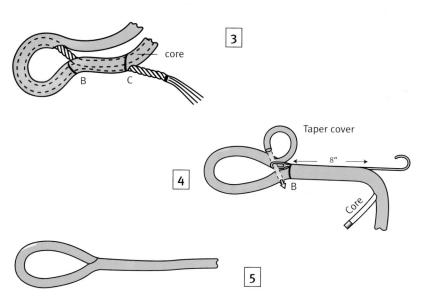

between marks B and C as much as you can, and insert a splicing tool or long wire loop, into the cover at mark C and out at mark A, taking great care not to snag any of the core. Pull the tapered core into the cover at mark A and out at mark C. Now taper the cover—this now has to fit into an already tight cover, so it is important that you bunch up the cover from mark C to mark B as much as possible. Insert the tool or wire loop into the cover about 8 inches (20 cm) from mark B then out at mark B. Pull the cover into the core—you may find it easier to do this in two or three stages, putting the tool into the cover at different points each time. Finally, attach the knot to a strong point, put a fid or handle through the eye and give it several sharp jerks to bed the splice in.

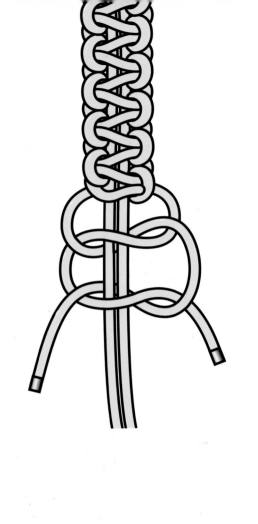

Knotcraft

Introduction

This final section of the book will take the reader into more intricate forms of knotting and ropework. Many knots, while still serving some practical purpose, are often used to make artistic, functional, or decorative creations. We start with Macramé, which was a popular craft in the 1970s, then sadly declined due partly to a lack of cost-effective materials. However, some people still use it to convert a few simple knots into an art form that can be used for all manner of coverings, adornments, and useful articles.

A small selection of plaits and sennits (braids) follows—these are used to make up flat or round decorative ropes for anything from plaiting hair to simple bell ropes. Examples of some two dimensional knots, used to make mats, coasters, or even necklace adornments, follow.

No knotting book would be complete without at least a few Turk's Head Knots, and to these I have added some of the so called "Marlinspike" or "Sailor's" knots, before ending the section with knots used for covering ropes or cylindrical objects for either decoration or protection.

Macramé

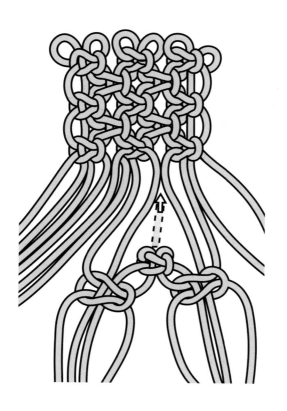

Introduction

Although the popularity of Macramé has dwindled since the 1970s, the use of Macramé and Cavandoli knot forms has survived in a surreptitious way and can be found on the covering of many a walking stick, bottle, handle, or even picture frame.

In this sub-section you will find only the methods of knotting used in Macramé—the way you then apply them is left to your imagination and creativity. Cord is expensive and you will not want to waste more than is necessary, so I have opened the section with some advice on how to estimate the amount of cord required—and although this is only one knot arrangement, it applies equally to the others.

There is then an introduction to some Cavandoli knots. Although Cavandoli is a knot form in its own right, it has long been considered an essential part of Macramé. The knotted bars that follow are also used in another knotting pastime known as Scoubidou or Boondoggle, which is popular with children.

Finally there is an introduction to Square Knotting, which forms a flat covering and can be designed to create all manner of different designs, to cover anything from a thin walking stick to a huge bottle, or even to make clothing and bags.

Sampler

In Macramé, where a large amount of cord is to be used, it is advisable to calculate how much it will take to complete a job; not only because you will not want to end up with too short a lead, but because most cord is expensive, so you will not want to waste any. The Macramé "Sampler" is the best way of finding this out.

Here is just a small part of a sampler to calculate the length of cord needed to do Square Knotting—other small samplers should be made to estimate different forms of knotting and for combinations of different knots, depending on your design ideas for the job in hand. A different sampler will be needed for each size of cord. If you cannot keep these, you should make a careful note in a "knotting workbook" for future reference. Macramé, Square Knotting, and Bars are all based on FOUR lengths of cord or multiples of four.

Shown in the example here are six ⁵⁄₃₂ inch (4 mm) diameter cords, each exactly 3 feet, 3 inches (1 meter) long. These are attached to a "bearer" at their center point with Lark's Head Knots, giving two leads each about 20 inches (50 cm). Using four of these, make up a sample of Square Knotting to suit your needs then take the measurements shown. Note the ends do not always remain the same length, so measure the shortest end—also note that, if you are edging by the method shown, the cords of the outside knots end up at very different lengths, so you can allow for this in your end cord.

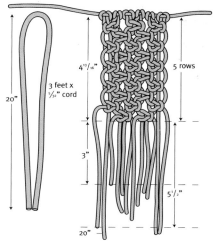

20"

3 feet x ⁵⁄₃₂" cord

4¹³⁄₁₆"

5 rows

3"

5¹⁄₂"

20"

Lark's Head Mounting

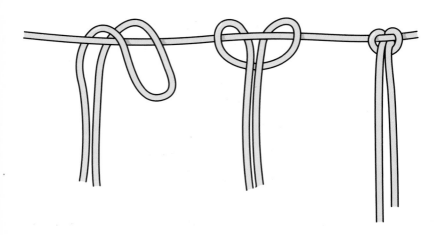

Fix the two ends of a horizontal bar or cord between two secure points on a board. An ideal Macramé
working board is about 12 inches (30 cm) across and 18 inches (45 cm) long—a piece of ply covered
with a cork tile or even a piece of Bristol board will suffice, so long as you can put pins into it. Screw
two small round eyes into the board about 10 inches (25 cm) apart and 1 inch (2.5 cm) from the top—
this will suffice to hold a thin bar. Alternatively, you can tie the two ends of a mounting cord to them.
Measure and cut your vertical cords then mount them one by one on the horizontal using the Lark's
Head Knot as shown in the diagram. The choice of having the collar of the knot at the front or the back
is yours—and will no doubt be influenced by your design for the final object. Another method of
mounting the start of the work is explained later on the Square Knotting pages.

Clove Hitch Bars

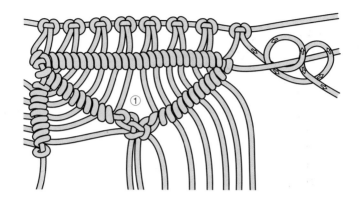

To form a horizontal knotted bar, take the left (or right) hand vertical cord and bring it across the work parallel to the last horizontal knotting (in this case the mounting Lark's Heads) — pin this to your board on the right hand side. Now with the next vertical cord apply two Half Hitches, in the same form as a Clove Hitch — as seen on the right of the diagram. Continue across the work until a complete line is achieved. To double this, take the last cord (in this case the one showing the Clove Hitch) and bring that horizontally across the work and pin it to the board — work across from right to left. To form a diagonal bar, the same procedure is employed except that the bearer cord is pinned at an angle to the last row of work OR if you fill the space (1) with Square Knotting, pin the cord close to the angle formed by the filling work.

A vertical bar is made by forming Clove Hitches around a vertical cord. A good tip to make this kind of knotting faster is to practice making the Half Hitches by tying the two cords in a Half Knot, then, holding the bearer, pull up on the other one — you will soon get the hang of it.

Solomon Bars

Shown here is another Sampler, and method of tying, with an alternative for making lanyards, etc.

Mount two doubled cords on to a horizontal bar or cord. Attach the mounting cord to the work board.

Now tie a Half Knot as shown in diagram 1—left behind the bearer, right under/over/under to the

left—right behind the bearers, left under/over/under to the right. You will now have formed a Square

Knot with the bearers trapped in the middle. By tying each half knot in the same direction (forming

Granny Knots), a spiral shape emerges like the one shown in diagram 3. Continue for the length of the

sample, then measure your ends and lengths as described on page 247.

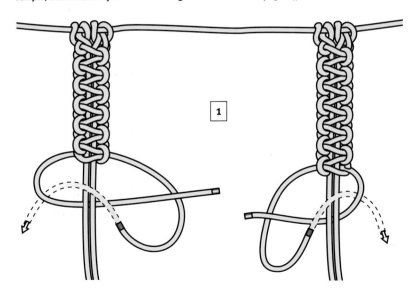

1

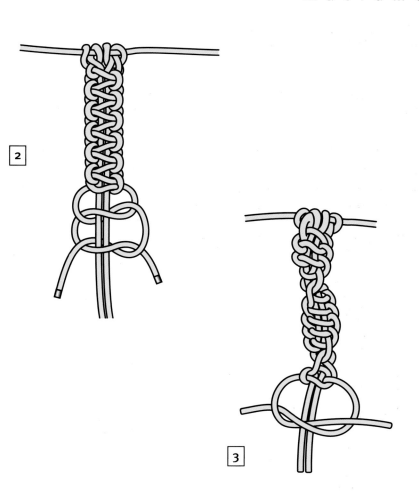

Solomon Bars Variation

The Solomon Ball is formed by opening up a knot between its center bearers four or five knots up from the last Square knot, as shown in diagram 1. Thread the two working center bearers through this opening, then the two side leads through the side strands in the same knot. Pull them up tight and continue with the knotting as before, forming a ball as shown in diagram 2.

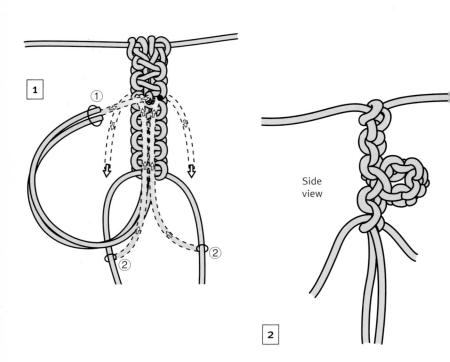

1

2

Side view

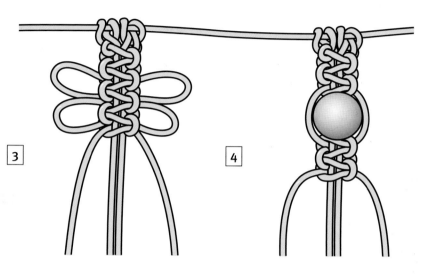

3 **4**

The wings are formed simply by pulling loops out sideways between two complete Square Knots. To insert a bead, take a bead of an appropriate size and, making sure the center hole is large enough, thread the center bearers through the bead, then continue knotting below the bead, as shown in diagram 4.

Square Knotting (Mesh)

Square Knotting can, when the Square Knots are joined in alternate rows, form a very attractive mesh or net. An alternative method of starting is shown here, and although this is not shown, it is advisable to thread a temporary horizontal bearer cord through the top loops to make the job easier. A fellow IGKT member, Ken Elliot, who is known for his bottle covering, showed me this method of starting and expanding Square Knotting.

1

Form two ears with the center bight of two cords, then with the two outer leads tie a Square Knot over the verticals as shown in diagram 1. Make enough of these to complete the width of the work or to go around the top of a bottle or jar etc. Now join them together with a second row of Square Knots, as shown in diagram 2, continuing until the row is complete, or you have joined all the verticals around a cylindrical object. When each row is complete, carefully pull each of the knots up with an even tension, and then pull the center bearers of the knot to form a neat diamond opening above

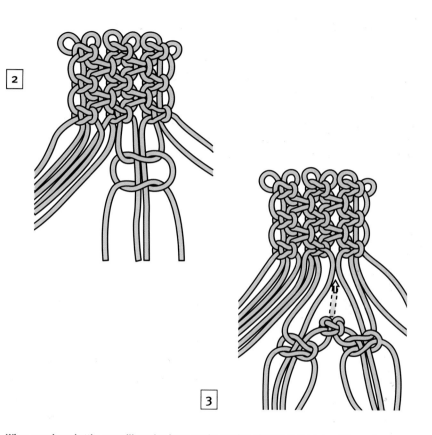

When covering a bottle, you will need to increase the number of leads at the base of the neck, as you are working towards a bulbous center. To do this, make additional verticals without the ears, then add them to the work as shown in diagram 3—you will hardly notice they are there.

Josephine Knot

The so called Josephine Knot is in fact a form of Carrick Bend and was published as far back as 1866 by Tom Bowling who called it a "Check Knot." The difference from a true Carrick Bend is that the two ends of the Josephine Knot emerge on the same side (see page 74).

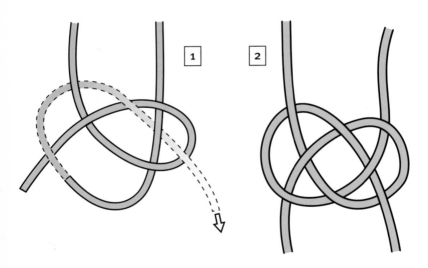

Make a crossing loop with one cord, then pass the other one across the loop on the same side as the working end of the other—in the diagram it is shown as being under the loop. Now complete the "over/under/over" sequence and tidy up the knot to look symmetrical. Diagram 3 shows how a series of these knots can be put together to form a chain, and diagram 4 shows the knot doubled.

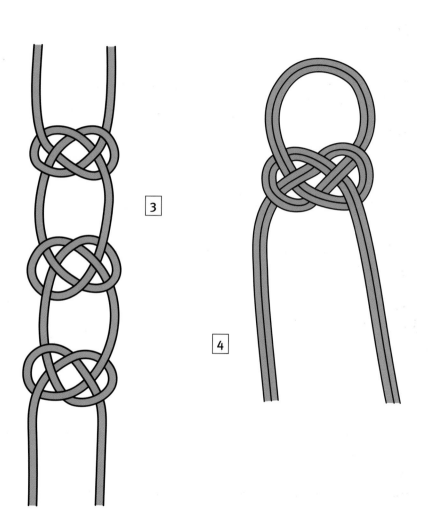

3

4

Simple Braids and Plaits

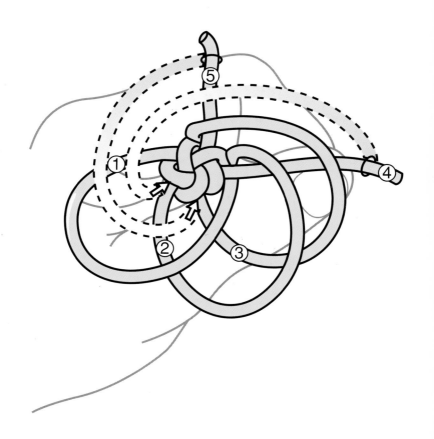

Introduction

In this section we cover a few simple plaits and sennits (or braids), which in turn can form parts of other knot structures. We start with a simple single strand plait that looks like three strands, with which we can turn a single cord into a plaited headband or hatband by tying the two ends together and teasing them into a small tassel.

Another example is the Six Strand Flat Plait—this can be made up single or doubled to decorate a picture frame. Among the sennits is an Eight Strand Round Sennit, on which you can base the shank of a bell rope or curtain pull.

All these are quite easy to make and can look quite attractive; however, the key to making plaits and sennits look good is even tension all the way through the knot—so don't be afraid to undo your work if a part does not look right the first time.

Single Strand Plait

This Single Strand Plait is one of many variations, each of which gives similar results. This one is chosen because the start is easy to remember—it is a Figure of Eight Knot.

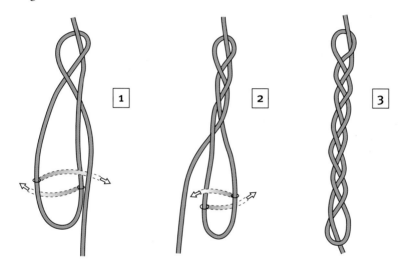

Tie a Figure of Eight knot, with the two end bights at a distance just a little more than the length of braid you require. Lay the knot out as in diagram 1, then turn the bottom bight over to the right and make a tuck with the working end, leaving it out to the left. The end is now on the left, so turn the bight to the left, and make another tuck with the working end. The end is now to the right, so turn the bight to the right and so on until you reach the end of the plait. The number of turns and tucks you make in a given length will determine whether the plait is open (as in diagram 3) or closed up more like a hair plait.

Three and Four Strand Flat Plait

The Three Strand Plait (diagram 1) is perhaps the most commonly used to plait hair, be it on a horse or human—it has always been seen as a neat way of controlling hair, apart from making it look nice. It fairs equally well in cord.

The three strands are gathered together at the top, then the plaiting sequence is: right over center, left over center, right over center, and so on. This can be finished off using a small whipping, or even a three strand Matthew Walker knot, the ends of which can be teased out into a tassel.

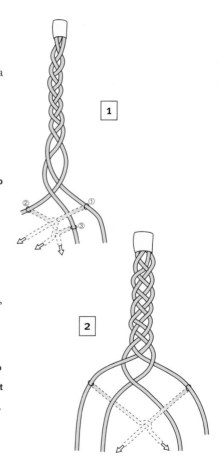

The Four Strand Plait shown here is, strictly speaking, a square plait, but if it is not pulled up too tight it will also lay flat.

Gather the four ends, then divide them into two on each side of the center line. Plait, outer right over one, hold to the left—outer left under one, over one, hold to the right—outer right over one, hold to the left, and so on in sequence.

Six Strand Flat Plait

This Six Strand Flat Plait is quite handsome when tied carefully—its main problem is in the starting and ending. It can also be tied using double strands, in which case it makes an attractive part of a picture frame decoration where the ends can be hidden under another knot or plait. Another solution for the ends (if the plait if going around a hat, for example) is to weave them into the plait and disperse the ends around the knot, gluing the ends together under a cross strand so that they are not too evident.

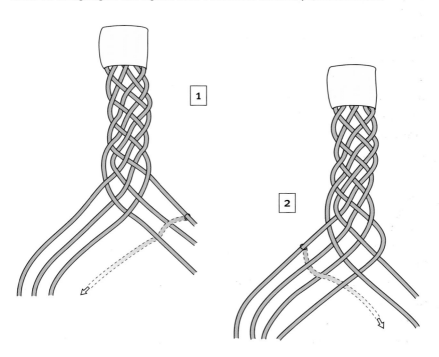

Round Crown Sennit

This Round Sennit is made from five strands—any more than six normally needs a core in the middle to stop it from collapsing. In this example the crowning is made by passing each lead over two adjacent leads—this has the advantage of holding better while the next layer is being built up.

Gather the five leads in the fist, as shown in diagram 1, then pass 1 over 2 & 3—2 over 3 & 4—3 over 4 & 5—4 over 5 and down through the loop made by 1—then 5 down through the loops made by 1 & 2. Pull the knot up tight—remember, even tension is the key to a good looking final knot. Look at diagram 2 and your knot should look like the one in the center. It may look complicated at first, but

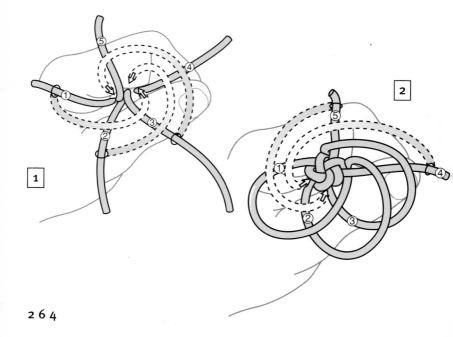

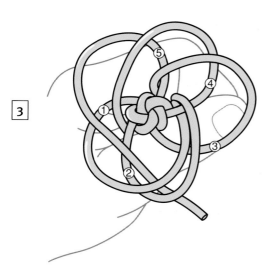

3

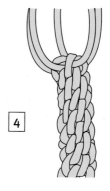

4

you will soon get the hang of it. On completion of the
next round of crowning your arrangement should look
like diagram 3. The end result should look like
diagram 4.

A Round Braid can also be made from three strands,
like the one in diagram 5, using the same knot as
depicted on page 40.

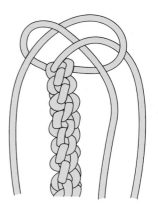

5

Square Crown Sennit *Also known as Nelson Plait*

This is an attractive square sennit that can be made with single strands, but looks much better with two or even three. It can be started from a previous four or eight lead knot to make up a lanyard or started from two or four doubled strands.

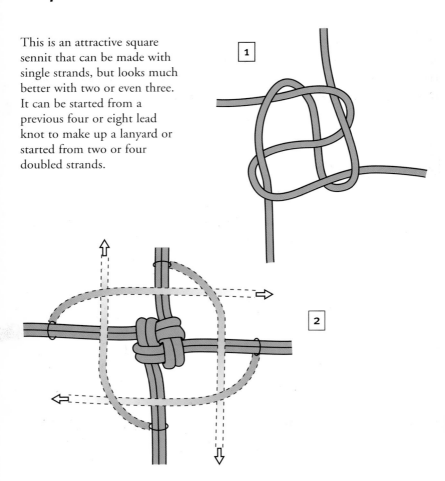

To start, double the strands and cross them in the middle; crown the leads to the right, then pull them up snug until they lock—diagrams 1 and 2 show single and double lead examples. Having made the first crown to the right, make the next to the left. This brings the leads back over themselves, as shown in diagram 3. Follow by crowning right and left alternately until sufficient length has been made.

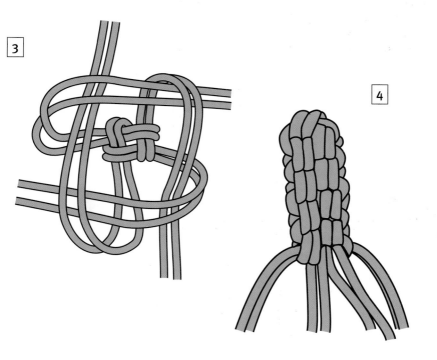

Eight Strand Round Sennit

An attractive braid that looks like stranded rope can be achieved with the Eight Strand Round Sennit. And it does not need a core, because it is made up from two sets of four leads, crowned, one on top of the other.

Start with eight strands—lay them out at 45 degrees to each other. Four alternate leads will be set (1) the other four will be set (2) – tie an Overhand Knot in the ends of one set so that you can easily identify them. Crown set (1) to the right (or left) and pull up snug—tuck these down in your holding hand. Each lead of set (2) must now be made to emerge from between two leads of set (1) – crown these to the right (or left) and pull up snug over the top of the first crown. Continue crowning alternate sets until the required length is achieved. Remember—even tensioning of every strand is the key to a good looking sennit.

Drummer's Plait *Also known as Chain Shortening*

You are most likely to see this plait on the drums of a military band, but it has many other uses, both practical and ornamental. Two practical uses of this plait include shortening a rope without having to cut it and making up a rope for stowage if it will not coil in the conventional way.

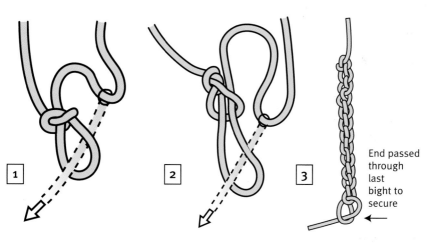

End passed through last bight to secure

To make the plait, start with a Slipped Overhand Knot—as shown in diagram 1—then pull a bight through the loop. Pull on this bight until the first loop closes up (not too tight), then pull the next bight through the second loop. Repeat as necessary until the required length is achieved. If you now pull on the working end the whole knot will come undone, like a zipper (which is one of the advantages of this arrangement). To prevent this from happening, pass the working end through the last loop and pull up snug.

Flat Knots

Latin Cross

Flat or two dimensional knotting, like this Latin Cross—shown to me by the late Brian Field, is often associated with Celtic Knots, but has also been used for many years to make other decorative knots, mats, and even jewelry. Many of these knots are made by pinning them out on a cork board; however, this one can be made in the hand.

The cross is made using two lengths of cord, which are doubled and laid out with the bights

uppermost in a Four Strand Plait arrangement, as shown in diagram 1.

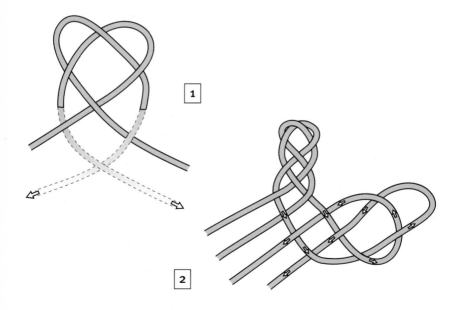

Make one more set of crossings, then take the upper right lead and form a crossing loop as shown in diagram 2—now weave the other lead emerging from the right through the loop as shown, checking that you end up with an "under, over, under, over" sequence. Repeat this for the left hand side, as shown in diagram 3. Pull up the resulting arrangement to look like the top of diagram 4, then continue down the vertical part of the cross.

There are two options to finish this cross. Either tuck the ends back as shown in diagram 4 and glue them behind the leads a short distance up the cross. Alternatively, take the same initial route, double the whole cross all the way up to the top and use the ends to hang the cross by—two long ends tied with a Double Fisherman's Knot will also form a necklace.

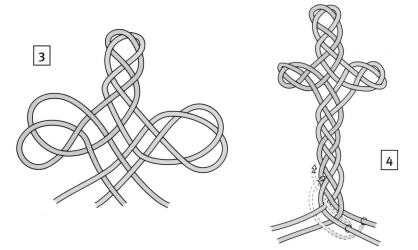

Ocean Plait Mat

The Ocean Plait Mat is a simple weave oval mat that can be made in cord or rope of up to about ¾ inch (18 mm) diameter. One word of warning before you start making mats with rope—a mat like this made in ½ inch (12 mm) rope can take as much as 115 feet (35 meters) to complete. Therefore, I make table mats with new cord, but I make floor mats only with old, used, or condemned rope!

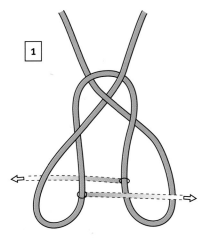

1

Take your cord/line/rope according to the size of mat you are making and find the center; make a bight with this and lay it out as shown in diagram 1—the bights of the lower loops need to be about the length of the mat you want to achieve.

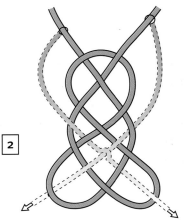

2

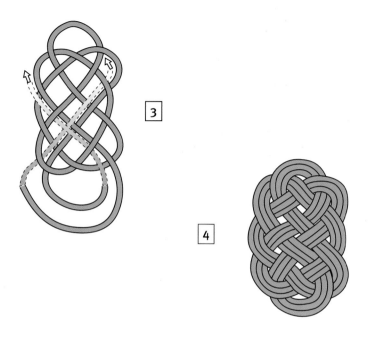

3

4

Move the left loop over the right and the right loop under the left to achieve the arrangement shown in diagram 2. Now take the top right hand end and weave it through the knot as shown— under/over/over/under. Take the top left end and weave that over/under/over/under/over, as shown. This now completes the weave and you can proceed to double or triple the passes, using each end in turn, following the previous lead. Cut the ends off adjacent to each other and sew or glue to the underside of the mat, out of sight.

Square Mat

This rather attractive Square Mat can be made without having to be pegged or pinned out first.

Halve the length of rope and tie a Half Knot in the bight, shaping it like a heart, as shown in diagram 1. Take the left hand end and weave it through the knot in an over/under/over weave, in the opposite weave to the leads in the Half Knot. At the position shown in diagram 2 pass the end, over/under/over/under, out of the top of the knot, then bring it back inside itself over/under/over/under, until it emerges alongside the other end.

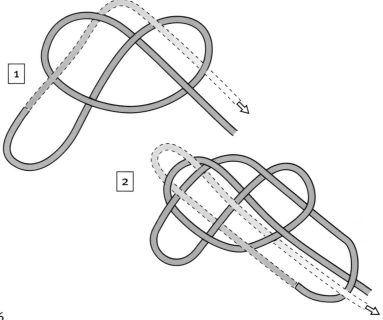

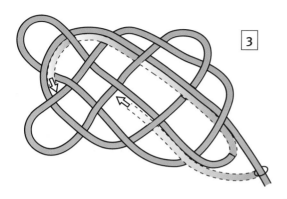

3

4

Now feed it into the knot on the left side of the other end and begin the second pass. Stop at this point and arrange the mat so that it is square and the bights around the edge are even and the same size. Continue doubling until you run out of rope, then use the other end in the opposite direction to complete the mat. Cut the ends off adjacent to each other and sew or glue them to the underside of the mat, out of sight.

Sailor's Breastplate *Also known as Round Mat*

From tiny clothing adornments to big rope "thump mats" (used on decks to prevent damage by blocks) this Round Mat design (as you will learn later), is in fact a Turk's Head, laid flat.

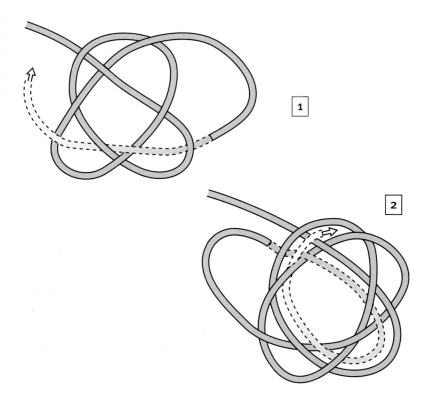

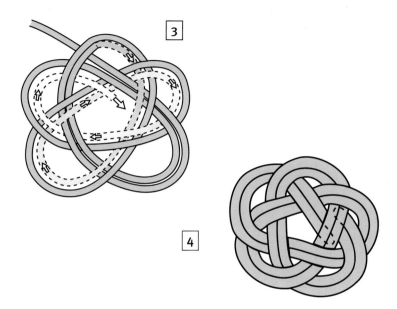

Double the rope, and with the bight uppermost, arrange it as in diagram 1. Taking the right hand upper lead, weave it through the knot in the direction shown—under/over/under/over—then back into the knot beside the other end and to its right. The knot is now formed and should be adjusted so that all the bights are even sizes and the knot looks symmetrical. Continue weaving the first end through the knot to double the lead. When the first end has been used up, take the other end and weave that back through the knot in the opposite direction until the required number of passes has been made complete. Cut the ends adjacent to each other and stitch or glue them to the underside of the mat, out of sight.

Turk's Head and Marlinspike Knots

Introduction

"Fancy Ropework" would be another way of introducing the knots in this section. Although, for many reasons, no longer a pastime for the sailor at sea, the artistic knotting that our old seafarers were known for has survived in some walks of life, and quite often you will see a post, walking stick, bell rope, or other cylindrical object decorated with one or more of the knots in this section. The Turk's Head can be made in literally hundreds of different combinations of leads and bights, by expanding the basic knots.

Shown here are three knots, which will teach the basic formation of the knot and at the same time introduce you to the principles of expanding these knots. Many a Turk's Head Knot has served as a Scout neckerchief woggle, or to decorate a post or stick—often to cover up the ends of other work, like Coach Whipping (page 306). The next knot, the Spanish Ring Knot, looks much nicer in leather than cord and is a very popular design for making bracelets.

It is said that if you can master the Star Knot you are a true knot tyer—learn here to handle a 5 point star, then progress to six, seven, or even more! One of the things people have problems with is how to end a plait, braid, or sennit—there is an example at the end of this section of how a Matthew Walker Knot can be used in this role.

Basic Turk's Head

Turk's Head Knots can become addictive, and having mastered the three elementary ones in this book, you may well want to consult other books (leather braiding books are an excellent source) to learn the more complex and bigger knots. So it is as well to start by learning a little about the structure of these now.

A Turk's Head Knot is usually formed with only one cord and is named after its structure—the one that is shown here (laid flat for illustrating purposes) is known as a Three Lead by Four Bight Turk's Head. This means that it has three leads; in other words it is like a Three Strand Plait arrangement and there are three leads across the knot. It has four bights around its edges, whether these be inside and outside as shown here, or left and right of the knot, as on page 285.

The other dimension (not reflected in the name) is how many times the cord is passed through the knot. These are called "passes" and are normally used to bulk it out or fill the gaps to give complete coverage over the article beneath.

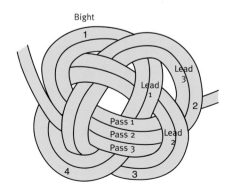

Three Lead x Four Bight Turk's Head of two passes with third pass commenced

Three Lead x Four Bight Turk's Head

The Three Lead x Four Bight Turk's Head is most commonly found used as a woggle on the neckerchief of a Scout, but it also looks nice on a walking stick or it can be used to cover the end of some hitching (pages 302–308) or other coverings.

To make a Three Lead x Four Bight Turk's Head with two passes, first estimate the amount of cord required, by winding it loosely around the object (or fingers) six times (3 x 2) and two more turns for handling. Start by making a crossing turn around the object back over itself, then tuck the working end under the standing part as shown in diagram 1. This is the first over/under crossing. Cross the top of the left hand turn over the top of the first turn. Then tuck the working end over and under the leads beyond the crossing as shown in diagram 2.

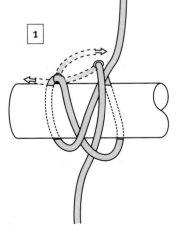

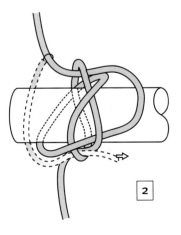

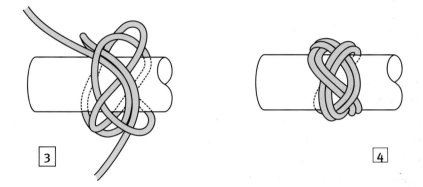

This should bring the end out where one more over pass will bring the two ends together. Continue around the knot on the left hand side (or right) of the original pass to make the second pass (or more). Tighten the knot a little at a time, starting from one end and working around the knot. After the first round, tuck the ends inside the knot and back out one or two leads from the point of entry. Continue pulling the knot up taut, taking care not to misshape it through over-tightening. Finally pull gently on each end and cut it off—it should shrink back under the knot out of sight. If you are making a woggle, cut the two ends adjacent to each other and sew or glue them to the back of one of the leads.

Five Lead x Four Bight Turk's Head

The more leads in a Turk's Head, the wider it becomes. This Five Lead by Four Bight Turk's Head makes a wider covering or a wider ring—an ideal knot to make napkin rings.

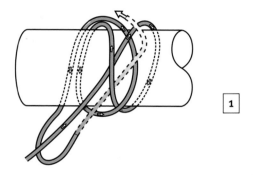

1

Start by estimating the length of cord required—this one will have three passes, so 5 x 3 = 15 loose turns plus a couple for handling. Make a crossing turn over the object, a mandrel or your fingers, and bring the working end back over itself and under the standing part. Take the working end into the knot on the right hand side of the standing part (this short part of the two lines together is known as "the pair"), following the sequence in diagram 1. At the top, go over the standing part, under the first crossing turn and around the back, ready for the next set of tucks. This is where we increase the size of the knot (from two leads to five leads) by "splitting the pair." Re-enter the knot between "the pair"

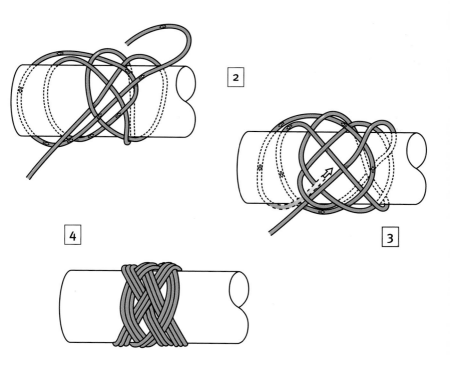

and weave the working end between them, but make the tucks the opposite way (where the standing part goes over, the working end goes under).

Continue the "over, under, over" sequence until the end emerges ready to make the second pass around the knot. Make the second and third passes and carefully pull the knot up nice and even, before gradually tightening it. After the first round, bury the ends and bring them out a couple of leads away, continue tightening and then cut the ends off so that they shrink back under the knot. For a napkin ring you will need to cut them inside and glue or stitch them to the underside of a lead.

Three Lead x Five Bight Turk's Head

We have seen how to increase the number of leads; this example of the Turk's Head will increase the number of bights, and will form the base knot for the Spanish Ring Knot on page 290. Estimate the length of cord required as before (leads x passes + 2).

Start the knot around a cylindrical shape with a crossing turn, bringing the working end up behind the standing part, over itself, then under the standing part again. This is in fact now a Two Bight Turk's Head that we will increase to five as follows—cross the left hand top bight over the right hand one, making sure you hold the second cross at the back of the work, or you will lose it.

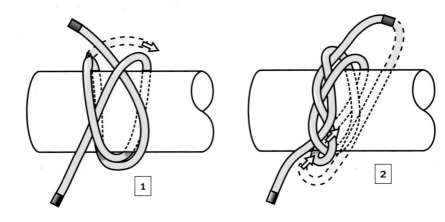

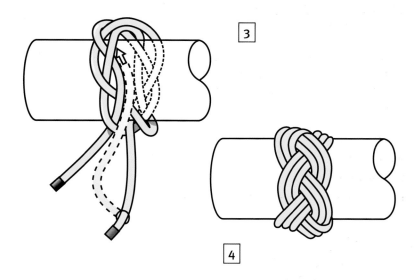

Weave the working end under the left lead beyond the first cross and over and out to the right. Now go

beyond the cross you held on the back and go under and over and out to the left again. Tuck the

working end back into the knot beside the standing part to complete the first pass. Continue for as

many passes as you have allowed cord. Finish by tucking the ends under the knot then working the

knot up neatly and gradually tightening it until it is firm—cut the ends to shrink back inside the knot,

or cut and stitch or glue them inside the knot.

Spanish Ring Knot

Traditionally the Spanish Ring Knot is used by leather braiders for belt loops or bracelets and similar rings, but it also works well in cord.

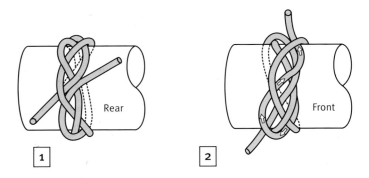

Estimate the leather or cord length by passing it around a suitable size mandrel nine times. Tie a Three Lead x Five Bight Turk's Head of one pass (pages 288–289), which should look like diagram 1. Take the working end over the top of the standing part; you will now see that it has gone "over two" (O2) leads at the bottom of diagram 2—this commences the first round of tucks with the sequence "over two (O2) under one (U1)." Continue to weave the working end U1/O2/U1/O2/U1, which should bring you out at the bottom of the knot as in diagram 3 (note this is the rear of the knot). The next pass will be an "over two,

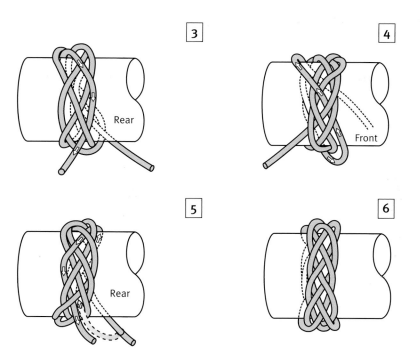

under two" sequence. Now weave the working end through the knot O2/U2/O2/U2/O2/U2. If you then

weave O2 again you should meet the standing part; if not, yes, go back to the start! Tuck the standing part

up alongside the working end and bury these ends under the knot, securing with a stitch or glue. Should

you wish to make a ring of a larger diameter, choose a larger mandrel and having made a Five Bight Turk's

Head, increase it to eight or eleven bights by adding left over right crosses, and the subsequent tucks,

then use the "O2, U1" sequence for the first pass and "O2, U2" sequence for the second.

Star Knot

Said to be the summit of fancy knotting, the Star Knot, because of its complexity, is quite a challenge to many. However, if the knot is tied carefully, step by step, and kept in neat order, it becomes quite an easy knot to master. A five point star is a good place to start; it can be tied with more, but if it is, it needs the support of a core. The knot will stand alone as a button or stud, but is more likely to be found in a bell rope separating one section from another.

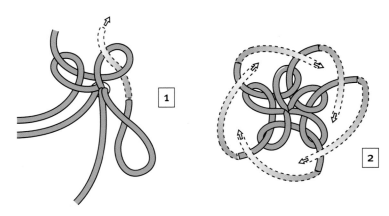

To tie, take five cords and hold them in a clenched fist, thumb on top, or tape them to a core. Twist a

crossing loop in the first cord and pass the next one up through it; twist a crossing loop in that one and

pass the next one up through that, as shown in diagram 1. The result should look like diagram 2. Crown

the ends to the left, over the top of the loops—pull up to look like diagram 3. Next, take one cord and

pass it alongside the one to its right until it goes down alongside it in a loop—take this end into your

hand so that you do not use it again. Take the cord that you have just followed and pass that in the

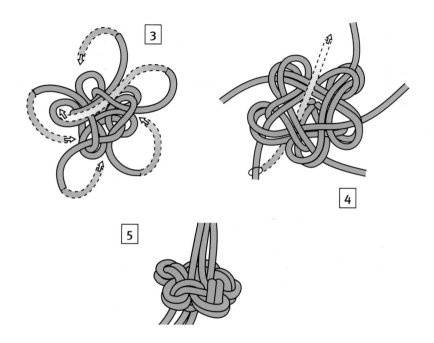

same manner beside the one to its right. Continue for all five cords; pull the knot up neat, but not tight yet. To complete the knot, pass each cord up through the center of the knot—if you turn it over the underside should begin to look like the final diagram. This knot now needs very carefully pulling up snug—if you pull too tight on the first points the others will be out of shape and difficult to rearrange. Start from where a cord emerges from the core and, using a blunt needle or spike, pull each one up in the sequence it was tied.

Matthew Walker Knots

No more than a collection of Half Hitches in reality, but the simplicity and symmetry of this knot is very pleasing to the eye. It has been covered in a previous section, but it appears again here because it has a place in the Fancy Ropework arena, in that it will create a knob in a rope—as shown in diagram 3—a knob of a tassel, or join a number of cords together at the end of another piece of knotting—as shown in diagram 2.

The three strand Matthew Walker Knot in a rope is tied as shown on page 198, then the rope laid up again.

1

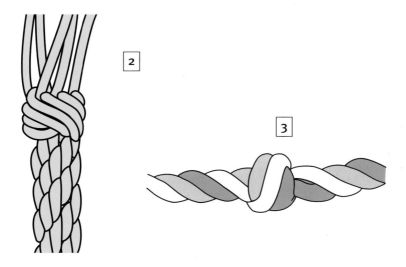

To tie a multiple strand Matthew Walker Knot, take the first strand and make a loop to the left, then pass the end around the work and up through itself. Take the next lead, make a loop to the left, then take the end behind the previous lead and up through both loops. The next and subsequent leads take the same route, around the work behind the previous lead and up through all the existing loops. This will result in an arrangement like diagram 1. Gather all the ends and move them, as one, up in line with the core. Gradually, very gradually, pull each end in turn—you will notice that when you pull an end it pulls up the bight to its right—go around the knot in sequence, laying the strands in place to form the knot in the final diagram.

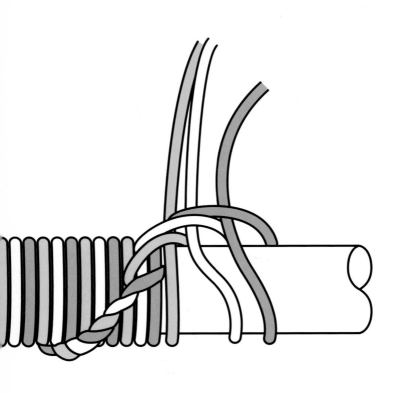

Knotted Coverings

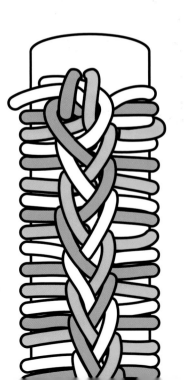

Introduction

Covering rails, handles, steering wheels, posts, and the like is primarily done to shield the bare hand from either heat or cold. But covering can also make a rail or handle "look good" too. The simplest covering is "Serving," and, although practical, it is not very decorative and so other knotted coverings have emerged over the years that create pleasing patterns as well as being practical.

This section starts with some advice on starting and ending coverings, in particular, Serving, but are adaptable for many other coverings. The next sequence shows Serving over a rail, as opposed to Serving over rope or wire, which employs the same principles, but needs more preparation. This is followed by two very quick and easy Half Hitch coverings, the French and Moku Hitching.

Then we show a fairly recent innovation by Brion Toss—his St Mary's Hitching, namely Half Hitching with three cords, the result of which looks like Serving with a rope spiral. For covering a ring or curved handle there is nothing better than "Cockscombing," which is another sequence of Half Hitching, but the hitches are bulkier than the wrap, which makes it unsuitable for covering straight cylindrical objects.

Another, more complex, covering is called "Coach Whipping," which creates an under/over woven pattern and can be executed in cord or cloth. Finally there are some ideas on how you can cover steel rods with stranded rope, or by using the cover of braided ropes, to make "rope" objects for the home or garden.

Starting and Ending

Starting and ending of "Serving" or other knotted coverings all too often end up by being whipped, or, even worse, glued to the rail and covered over with a Turk's Head to "hide the ends"—that is all well and good if you want to decorate the ends, but there are times when that is not appropriate.

Starting. Whenever you cover a rail, a yacht steering wheel, or in particular metal objects, it is advisable to cover them first with a cloth tape (the type climbers use for their fingers is suitable). This can be waterproofed for added protection against rust if you wish. Take the end of the cord and tease it out about 1¼ inches (2 cm) into a fan of yarns—tape the cord to the rail so that it will lay horizontally along the rail under about ten turns. Make the first turn by hand, keeping the first crossing as near to 90 degrees as possible (see diagram 1 on page 300), pull it up tight, then make the second turn and pull that up very tight. You can now proceed with the remainder of the covering.

Ending. At a distance of about ten turns from the end of the work, stop and insert a "heaving rope" as shown in diagram 2 (page 300)—a piece of cord about 3 feet (1 meter) long will suffice. Now lay a finger, pen, or, as shown, a Swedish Fid, along the rail and make the last ten, or so, turns over it. Pass the working end (which needs to be long enough to wrap around a bar or handle to pull on) back through the turns then pull each one up, in turn, hand tight. Go back to the heaving rope and lay back on it, then, maintaining the tension, pass it around the rail and lay back on it again—repeat until you reach the last turn. The end will be trapped under the turns and now has to be pulled up tight. This should require considerable effort, otherwise the final turns are too loose. Wrap the end around a bar with riding turns and jerk to pull the cord tight. Cut the end by holding a sharp knife blade against the cord, between two turns, then move the cord back and forth until it parts. Resist hot knives and sawing knife blade actions—they might damage your work.

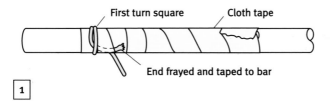

First turn square   Cloth tape

End frayed and taped to bar

1

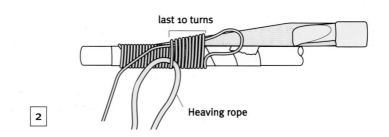

last 10 turns

Heaving rope

2

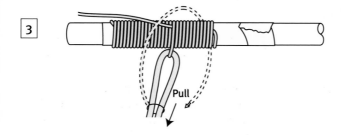

3

Pull

Serving

Serving is the term used when a line or cord is wrapped around a rope, wire, or rail in a continuous close spiral. In all cases it needs to be put on nice and tight. You have seen on the previous page how to start and end the Serving—now for the bit in between. Having made the first two turns by hand, you now need a suitable tool to apply an even tension to the work all the way along.

The conventional tool for this is the "Serving Board" or the "Serving Mallet," a wooden mallet with a groove in the head that fits around the rope, wire, or rail. Diagram 1 shows how this is used—the line is brought up in front of the head, around the handle, back across the head, around the rope, then wound around the handle. This now becomes a two-man job, one passing the mallet around the work, the other, "passing the ball" around the work in unison with the mallet. A homemade serving board of sorts can be made by drilling four holes, just slightly larger than the line, about 1¼ inches (30 mm) apart, in a piece of thick broom handle about 8 inches (20 cm) long.

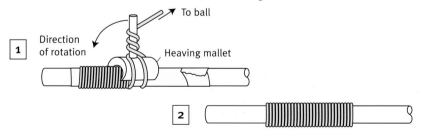

To use this, feed the line through the holes, from one side to the other then back through the next hole, before you attach it to the rail. Pass the handle around the rail at 90 degrees to it; the weave through the stick should provide enough tension on the line, but if not, take a couple of turns around it as well. This method also needs a second person to "pass the ball" of line. Finish the Serving as described on page 299.

French and Moku Hitching

French Hitching can be laid on by hand, and not require any tools. It provides a good close covering with an attractive spiral around the work.

Start the hitching as described on page 299, but instead of passing the first turn around the rail, make a Half Hitch to the right. The work now consists of continuous Half Hitching all the way to the end. Make each Half Hitch in turn, pull it tight, then pull it back on itself and check that it is tight before making the next Half Hitch and so on.

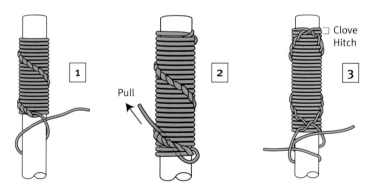

1

Pull

2

3

☐ Clove
Hitch

Moku Hitching is like a double French Hitching, where the spiral goes around the work in opposite directions then crosses over and diverges again (diagram 3).

This hitching is started by doubling the line and, at the center, making a Clove Hitch around the rail. Half Hitch each end in turn, as you would French Hitching until you get to the point where the knots cross. At this point make sure the hitch that goes to the left is on top of the one going to the right. Finish off using the method described on page 299 (without the heaving rope), leading both ends up beside the knotting so that they do not show.

St Mary's Hitching

St Mary's Hitching creates a neat rope-like spiral around what looks like Serving. It is shown here in three colors for illustrative purposes, but it looks equally good in a single color.

Start as on page 299, but with three cords. Half Hitch the left hand one to the right, the center one over the first to the right and the third over both to the right— pull each one up tight so that the knots lie back snug together. Now take the top one and hitch that over the two below it, repeating the tightening sequence all the way along the work.

This too can be finished using the method on page 302 (diagram 2), or the ends can be whipped to the rail if a Turk's Head is going to be used at the end of the work.

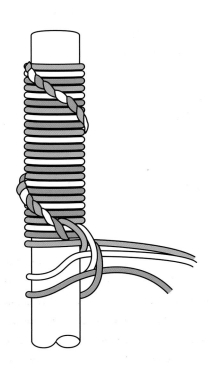

Cockscombing

Cockscombing is a traditional ring covering, but can be used on curved rails or handles too. If it is done on a straight rail, shown in the illustrations in order to make each step easier to follow, it leaves ugly gaps in the work. This is because the knot is larger than the diameter of the cord.

Start by taping three cords to the rail as in diagram 1. Take the left hand cord and half hitch it to the right, take the center cord and half hitch that to the left, then the right hand cord and half hitch that to the right. Now take the top cord and half hitch that to the left, and so on around the work. Pull each Half Hitch up tight and snug against its previous lead as shown in diagram 2.

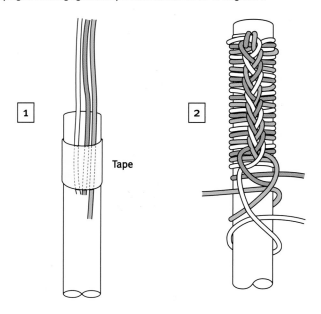

1

Tape

2

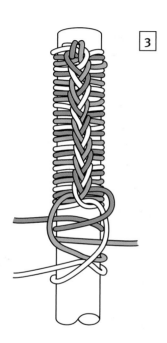

3

4

This knotting is then finished using a Double Constrictor Knot tied tightly over the ends—very close to the last Half Hitch—and the ends cut short. Work the two ends of the knotting together to cover the whipping and even the knotting around the ring.

Coach Whipping

Coach Whipping provides a neat closed or open weave under/over pattern around a cylinder. It can be laid in cord, line, or even strips of cloth. The method shown here is the basic form of Coach Whipping and the easiest to apply single-handed.

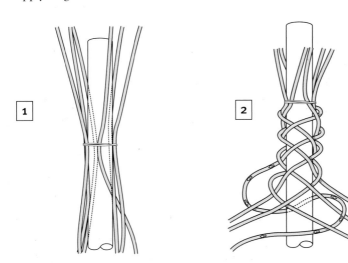

Take six cords, at least four times the length of the covering required. Mark the center of each cord and the center point of the area to be covered on the rail. Secure the six cords to the rail using a Double Constrictor Knot over the mark on the rail, adjusting each one so that the cord center mark is under the knot.

This will be the center of the final whipping. Take the three cords on the left in the left hand and the other three in the right hand. Commence a Six Strand Round Sennit—take the outer left around the back then under/over/under the cords on the right—return this to the left hand (diagram 2). Take the outer right cord

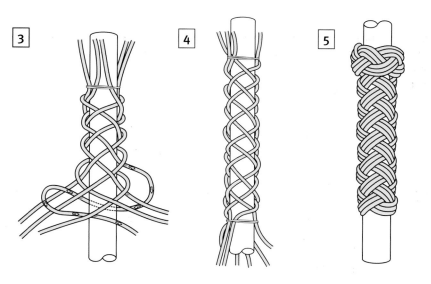

around the back then under/over/under—return this to the right hand (diagram 3). Continue to the end of the whipping area and secure the cords temporarily with a Constrictor Knot. Turn the work around and work from the center to the other end in the same manner. Your work should now look like diagram 4 with the center knot removed. The base knot is now complete. To triple the knot—at one end take two leads that look as though they are about to cross and pass one up inside the other into the knot. The other then goes outside it into the knot; continue to follow the weave to the other end. Do the same with each pair, then repeat the process at the other end. The ends can now be fed back into the knot, removing the corresponding lead as you go so as to bury them at different stages along the knot. Alternatively, whip the ends to the rail and cover with a Turk's Head, as shown in diagram 5.

Rope Covering

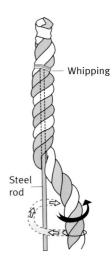

Whipping

Many everyday items (e.g. barbecue lantern stands and long hooks to hang bird feeders) are made up of 8–10 mm steel rods, and they can be covered using this method. Attractive rope arches for the garden can be made by bending a length of ⅜ inch (10 mm) steel rod and covering with stranded rope.

Steel rod

To do this, tape or whip the end of the rope securely, place the rod into the lay of the rope and carefully twist the rope against the lay to partly un-lay it, then spiral it around the rod and snug it up. Put a very tight whipping at both ends and cover with a Turk's Head. Cut the ends about ⅛ inch (3 mm) from the whipping. If both ends are to go in the ground, start by laying the rope on the rod about 12 inches (30 cm) from the end and apply a very tight whipping, leaving about 12 inches (30 cm) of rod at the other end as well.

Rope covers on thin cylindrical objects can enhance their looks and provide a better grip or just be a talking point! Take any cheap ballpoint pen, most of which are around ⁵⁄₁₆ inch (8 mm) in diameter, and then cut a length of ⅜ inch (10 mm) braided rope outer cover and heat seal the ends.

Hold the pen in one hand, the braid in the other, and push the braid so that it

Push to bunch   Push to insert

Min rope size ⅜ inch (10 mm)   Pen ⁵⁄₁₆ inch (8 mm) diameter

bunches up, then push the pen into the braid. When the pen is covered down to the taper, apply a whipping to the cover as shown. The top can be bent over to look like a clip and sewn or glued to the shaft or cut square at the top and whipped using a fancy whipping or hitching—or maybe a Turk's Head.

Glossary

Becket—rope, cord, or tape formed to make a handle or securing point.

Belly—of a knot; the part of the knot that joins two ends of tucks before being pulled up.

Bend—verb used to describe the action of knotting two ropes together.

Bight—any part of a rope between the two ends, especially when slack and bent back on itself to form a loop. A knot tied "in the bight" or "on the bight" does not require the ends for the tying process.

Binding—the tying with line around two or more objects to hold them tightly together.

Braid—yarns (normally very fine) woven together to form a band, cover, or decoration.

To Braid—is to form a braid with knotting, normally in the hand or on a Maru Dai, or other specifically made formers.

Breaking strain or strength (BS)—the rope manufacturer's calculation of the average load that will cause an unused rope to break. (See also Safe Working Load (SWL), which can be as little as 6 percent of the BS.)

Bungee—a line of elastic rubber yarns, bound and held by a man-made fiber stretching cover—also known as "shock cord."

Cable—a large rope, anchor warp (q.v.), or chain.

Cable laid—rope formed of three right-handed hawsers laid up left-handed to form a larger nine-stranded rope or cable.

Capsize—verb used to describe the change in the form of a knot. This can either be accidental—where stresses are applied to a loose or wrongly pulled up knot causing the knot to become insecure; or deliberate—when forces are applied to parts of the knot to make it easier to untie.

Capstan—A drum, normally vertically mounted on the deck of a ship, around which rope, wire, or chain is "hauled in" using motorized or hand power.

Cavandoli—the art of making objects of clothing or decoration by the use of horizontal and vertical bars of hitching.

Cleat—a wood or metal fitting having two horns, to which ropes are belayed.

Coach Whipping—the over/under/over pattern of knotting used for covering cylindrical objects. May also be executed with strips of cloth, canvas, or tape.

Glossary

Cord—the name given to several tightly twisted or plaited yarns (q.v.) to make a line with a diameter of less than ⅜ inch (10 mm).

Cordage—a collective name for ropes and cords.

Core or **Heart**—the inner part or heart of a rope or sinnet (q.v.) of more than three strands and in most braided lines; it is formed from a loosely twisted strand or from a bundle of parallel yarns or plaited strands and runs the length of the rope. It may be just a filler or may serve specifically as the main strength bearer in braided ropes.

Dog/Dogging—the act of whipping together the ends of two separate strands of rope to prevent them from pulling out.

Double line—similar to a loop (q.v.), but both parts of the line are used together rather than working with the loop that is formed.

Dress—to tighten and form a loosely tied knot into its final shape.

End—usually the end of a length of rope that is being knotted, but see *standing end* and *working end*.

Eye—a loop formed at the end of a length of rope by knotting, seizing, or splicing— see *Hard Eye*. Also an aperture in a hook, thimble, or needle through which a line can be threaded.

Fender—soft rope, rubber, or plastic arrangement, used on the side of a vessel to prevent damage by dockside fittings or other vessels when alongside.

Fid—a tapered wooden pin or hollow metal spike, used to work or loosen strands of a rope, especially when splicing.

Foul—describes a rope that cannot slide because it is tangled or caught.

Frapping turns—those turns around a lashing that serve to tighten it before securing the end.

Fray—verb used to describe the unraveling, especially of the end, of a length of rope.

Grapevine method—an alternative method of tying multiple Overhand Knots, when made around a second standing rope or part.

Grommet—a ring of rope, made up using one strand laid around itself three times.

Guardrail—wire, rope, or steel tubing rove through stantions around the edge of a deck, to guard against people and objects falling from it.

Guy lines—stays of rope or wire that serve to hold objects in position.

Hard Eye—a spliced eye that contains a thimble or round eye of metal or polymer construction so as to prevent undue wear on the rope from shackles and fittings.

Hard laid—tightly laid up rope—tends to be stiff and difficult to knot or coil.

Harness—term used to describe an arrangement of rope, leather, or webbing worn on the body. Normally used with lines attached to provide suspended seating, to attach tools, or to prevent accidental falling.

Hawser—a rope or cable large enough for towing or mooring.

Heart—see *core.*

Heaving line—a light line, typically 5/16 inch (8 mm) diameter and about 100 feet (30 meters) long, with a Monkey's Fist or Heaving Line Knot on the end as a weight.

Hitch—a knot that secures a rope to a post, ring, spar, etc. or to another rope.

Hobble—rope or tape used to tether one or more of the feet of a domestic animal.

Hot Knife—an electric (or gas) heated blade, used to cut and seal the ends of man-made fiber ropes.

Karabiner—a metal coupling link with a safety closure—used mainly for industrial roping, climbing, and caving.

Kernmantel—method of rope construction consisting of a core of filaments over which a tight outer sheath of braided fibers is fitted.

Lanyard—a short rope or cord, usually three stranded but can be braided or ornamented, used to secure objects; used for rigging; or used as a handle, safety line, or hanging loop for tools and equipment.

Lash/Lashing—term used when knotting over a loose article to hold it in place or bindings on poles, etc. to form frameworks.

Lay—the direction, either left- or right-handed, of the twist of the strands forming a rope.

Lay Back—term meaning to put all one's weight behind pulling a line or rope.

Lay up—re-laying the strands of a rope that have been unlaid, to restore the rope to its original form.

Lariat or **Lasso**—rope with a running noose, used to ensnare animals from horseback.

Lead—the direction taken by the working end (q.v.) through a knot.

Line—the generic name for cordage with no specific purpose, although it can be used to refer to rope with a definite use, e.g. fishing line, clothes line.

Glossary

Loop—a part of a rope bent so that its parts come together.

Macramé—the art of knotting with simple knots to decorate or make clothing, hangings, bags, belts, and coverings, etc.

Mandrel—a cylindrical rod or tube around which hollow knotting, such as Turk's Head Knots, bracelets, etc. can be formed while in the tying process.

Marline—a thin line of two strands, often loosely twisted, traditionally left-hand laid. Used for seizing, marling, etc.

Marling—the act of lashing or binding with marline (q.v.), taking a hitch at each turn.

Marlinspike—a round, pointed metal instrument for separating the strands of a rope (especially wire) when splicing or for use as a lever to tighten seizing.

Marry—to bring two ropes together so that they can be worked as one.

Messenger—a light line/rope used to haul the end of a larger, heavier rope from one point to another. Typically used between a heaving line and berthing hawser.

Monofilament—a single fiber of one of the polymers that has no joins.

Mooring—the term used for attaching a vessel to a fixed object—typically by anchor or to berthing facilities.

Multi-plait—strong but flexible rope that does not kink, plaited using four or six pairs of strands, half of which are right-hand laid, the other half left-hand laid.

Nip—the binding pressure within a knot that prevents it from slipping.

Noose—a loop formed by the working end being tied around the standing part of a rope in such a way that, when the standing part is pulled or the loop pulled away from the standing part, it draws up tight.

Nylon—original common term for Polyamide

Pass—to follow the path of a lead around a knot with the working end again.

Pick—term used to denote one element of the weave in braided rope covers.

Prussik—sliding knot used on a static climbing rope. Now often used to refer to climbing using any sliding knot.

Reeve—verb used to describe the act of slipping the end of a rope through a block, ring, or cleat (q.v.).

Riding Turn—when the round turns of a line on a winch/capstan or bollard are entrapped by the standing part laying over them.

Rope—general term used for cordage that has a diameter of more than ⅜ inch (10 mm). Also used to specify a rope—as in bell rope, guy rope, bolt rope, etc.

Rove—when a rope is passed through the aperture in a block, eye, fairlead, etc, it is said to be rove through the block, etc.

Safe working load (SWL)—the estimated load that can be placed on a rope without it breaking, given its age, condition, the knots used, and any shock loading. NB: safe working load may be as little as one-sixth of the manufacturer's quoted breaking strength (q.v.).

Scoubidou—the making of adornments by tying braids, plaits, sennits, etc. in hollow plastic pieces of line—mainly a pastime for children.

Secure—to belay a line such that it will not move—a knot is said to be secure if, when tied, no manner of shaking or use will inadvertently untie it.

Seizing—binding with turns of small stuff that secures two parts of the same rope together or one rope parallel to another rope.

Sennit or **Sinnet**—braided cordage made in flat, round, or square form using three or more strands.

Serving—a binding in small stuff, twine, etc. Used particularly over wire rope splices.

Shear Legs—two poles, joined at the top with a lashing and spread apart at the bottom—for use as a frame to support or lift heavy objects.

Slack—the part of a rope that is not under tension.

S-laid rope—left hand laid stranded rope.

Sling—a rope or tape joined at the ends to form a loop that can be attached to a fixed point or static line to act as a suspension loop.

Slipped—the passing of a bight, rather than an end, to complete a knot whereby it can be untied by pulling the bight free.

Small stuff—twine, string, line or cord (q.v.) with a diameter of less than ⅜ inch (10 mm).

Snug—where two or more leads, or parts of a knot, are close up against each other to form a knot as it will be used.

Soft laid—loosely laid up rope, making it soft and supple.

Spill—the accidental untying of a knot.

Splice—verb used to describe the act of joining the ends, or the end and a standing part, of rope by interweaving strands.

Square Knotting—another term for Macramé.

Standing part—the part of a rope that is fixed or under tension as opposed to the end that is free (the working end) with which the knot is tied.

Stop—a binding knot or whipping used as a temporary measure to stop a rope from unraveling.

Stopper—a short length of rope or chain, secured at one end, used to control the running or for securing another rope.

Stow—to place an article in its proper place of storage when not in use.

Strand—yarns twisted together in the opposite direction to the yarn itself; rope made with twisted strands (not braided) is known as laid line.

Tag end—the part of a fishing line in which the knot is tied; see *working end*.

Temporary whipping—the use of tape or a binding knot to form a "Stop."

Turn—one 360 degree path taken by a rope around an object or when coiled. To "take a turn" is to make a single round with the rope around an object such as a cleat or bollard.

Unlay—to separate the strands or yarns of a rope.

Weave—the in/out or under/over pattern formed by interlacing strands or cords.

Webbing—woven strapping—often used for slings or strops.

Whipping—the act of tightly wrapping small stuff around the end of a length of rope to prevent it from unlaying and fraying.

Working end—the part of the rope used in tying a knot—the opposite of standing part (q.v.).

Yarn—a number of fibers twisted together.

Z-laid—right handed rope.

Index

Index

Author & Further Reading

THE AUTHOR

Gordon Perry has been knot-tying now for some 60 years. Initially as a member of the Cubs, Sea Scouts, and Sea Cadet Corps in his home town of Margate, Kent, England, he also gained early knot-tying experience while shrimp trawling, lobster fishing, and angling with his father. Joining the Royal Navy as a boy at the age of 15, he went on to make this his long-term career, retiring as a Lieutenant Commander some 40 years later. During this time, apart from the practical use of knots, he practiced decorative ropework as a hobby. A long-standing member of the International Guild of Knot Tyers (IGKT), Gordon is a past editor of their magazine *Knotting Matters* and is currently the Guild Librarian and a Council Member. He has appeared on both television and radio programs. Now retired, he keeps busy doing commercial and bespoke knotting, splicing, and ropework; and by flying and smallbore rifle shooting. He was awarded the MBE in 1992.

The **INTERNATIONAL GUILD OF KNOT TYERS** has over 1200 members worldwide and all have a common interest in knotting—whether it is practical, theoretical, magic, artistic, creative, or inventive. Whatever your interest, there is someone here who can help you.

Log on to the IGKT website at www.igkt.net where you will find information about the Guild, a forum in which you can discuss your knotting problems, and help in selecting further reading.

On the site there is even a friendly "chat net," details of how to contact local branches, and links to many other knotting websites. Also published on this site are the dates and venues of Guild and Branch meetings, which you will be most welcome to visit if only to be inspired by the variety of members' work.